EXPLICIT COST
DYNAMICS

EXPLICIT COST DYNAMICS

An Alternative to Activity-Based Costing

Reginald Tomas Yu-Lee

John Wiley & Sons, Inc.

New York • Chichester • Weinheim • Brisbane • Singapore • Toronto

This book is printed on acid-free paper.

This publication is designed to provide accurate and authoritative information in regard to the subject matter covered. It is sold with the understanding that the publisher is not engaged in rendering legal, accounting, or other professional services. If legal advice or other expert assistance is required, the services of a competent professional person should be sought.

Library of Congress Cataloging-in-Publication Data

Yu-Lee, Reginald Tomas, 1964-
  Explicit cost dynamics: an alternative to activity-based costing/Reginald Tomas Yu-Lee.
    p. cm.
  Includes index.
  ISBN 0-471-38943-9 (alk. paper)
  1. Direct costing. 2. Cost accounting. I. Title.
  HF5686.C8 Y82 2001
  658.15'52—dc21

                                                              00-050978

Printed in the United States of America.
10 9 8 7 6 5 4 3 2 1

To my daughter, Erin, and my father, Rudolph

EXPLICIT COST DYNAMICS

Preface

I once was asked by a student if increases in productivity reduce costs. I basically blew off his question because the answer was obvious. Of course they reduce costs. His response was, "If no one was fired, how have we saved money?" I gave the stock answers, but as I tried to create that cloud of complexity often used to confuse students to the point where they give up hope, I realized that he was right. The ultimate question was, "Why was he right?"

Numerous debates, academic exercises, and consulting engagements have led to the development of explicit cost dynamics (ECD), a nonallocation cost management system that provides cost information based purely on bottom-line cost dynamics. With the bottom line as a basis, the implementation of ECD strives to provide decision makers with the relevant tools and information to understand the bottom-line impact of past, current, and future activities. It is the concept that ultimately proves why my student was right, for it eliminates the ambiguity created by allocating costs. It provides explanations regarding how to effectively bid on projects without allocating and still ensure the desired bottom line. It explains why a plant manager's approach is better for the company from a bottom-line perspective even though the accountant's measures suggested otherwise. As a cost management tool, it helps to explain why ideas such as Just-in-time manufacturing and Theory of Constraints seem to work, and it can explain why bad implementations of either will not work. It provides decision makers with the necessary information to operate their organizations without the confusion created by allocating costs.

Many different developments have led to creation of the ECD concept. First, while working for Business Dynamics & Research, I encountered an interesting scenario with a colleague. Our client, a wholesaler, won a large percentage of its bids below a certain dollar threshold. Above that threshold, it lost every bid over a given period of time, and we wanted to know why. We found that by allocating costs that existed regardless of whether they won the business or not, they overbid. By overbidding, they ended up getting nothing, which was not good since they had to pay the bills for the existing resources. We also did work for a client known nationally and perhaps internationally for its manufacturing and teamwork capabilities. It never made sense to me why the improvements that their amazing plant manager made caused the accounting numbers to suggest that the plant was not operating as well as it should. In reality, the plant likely outperformed almost any other manufacturing plant in the business with similar products.

While teaching, I looked into the fuss surrounding flexible and focused factories. Why did some propose that a flexible factory was more desirable, while the remaining group believed that a focused factory was the way to go? My conclusion was that the solution was based on what one was attempting to measure. If unit margins were being evaluated, the focused factory was often considered the best approach because each unit absorbed a very small amount of the fixed costs. The flexible factory offered advantages on the top end by providing more options to its clients, which leads to the ability to perform value pricing. The overall result was that depending, of course, on the market and the offering, providing more flexibility in pricing was a better approach. Why? Because the perceived savings from the focused factory were not always realized on the bottom line. With a standard product, flexibility in pricing was often not available. Although the measures required for flexibility may have driven up the costs of doing business, they could often offset this increase in cost through even greater increases in revenues.

While doing general consulting, in perhaps every engagement with which I have been involved, decision making was being driven not by the activities and the bottom line of the organization but by contrived measures based on principles that (as will be proven) do not reflect bottom-line cost dynamics. These include, for example, measures that employees can play with to make them look favorable. One situation in particular involved a plant manager who came into a vice president's office and asked, "What do you want this number to be?" This should be a major warning sign that the current approach of managing our organizations using these measures and techniques is wrong; it does not work, it leads to improper solutions and decisions, and it should be eliminated. We got rid of asbestos;

now lets get rid of measures, tools, and techniques that cause decisions to be made that few believe are right but are implemented anyway because of what the accounting measures predict.

All of this led to my search for a unifying cost management theory—one that explains why what we *know* is wrong, in fact, is wrong. ECD explains why those things that we intuitively think are right, in fact, are right. Many scholars have suggested that allocation does not work, and we now all do, or should, agree. The solution, however, often has been to create better allocation models rather than to eliminate the model altogether. We know that optimization models often lead to counterintuitive solutions. Why is this the case? Why do the short JIT runs work? Do smaller batches not lead to a higher unit cost? Well, yes, but who said that the unit cost was right? How do you know that you can even determine a unit cost? Why do I not see my productivity and efficiency improvements show up as cost savings on the bottom line? ECD will provide solutions to these and other questions by simply looking at the cost dynamics of an organization and building tools and measures around bottom-line cost dynamics to ensure that the bottom-line impact of every decision made will be known.

ECD is not meant to be a compliment to allocation-based accounting. It is meant to eliminate it. The purpose of this book, therefore, will be to introduce the concept and how it works and to open up the cost and management accounting world for debate. This is not a *how-to* book; nor is it a financial accounting book. It is an introduction to the concept and associated measures that will allow for more insight into the bottom-line cost dynamics of the organization. Although I would like to suggest that you can pick up the book and begin reading at any place, the reality is that there are some bold assertions and assumptions that are made in early chapters. Since subsequent chapters build on these assertions and assumptions, it is important for the reader to really understand the fundamentals first. Only then will the understanding and essence of ECD make themselves known.

Acknowledgements

There are a number of people who were instrumental in making this book a reality. I must first thank the members of my family whom I drove crazy while writing this book; Fred, Erin, Wynnette, Marc, DB, and Mi Hwa. My father unfortunately will never be able to read the book, but being an accountant, he was involved in shaping the concepts while in their primitive form. At least he was spared my driving him crazy too. Without the unending support of my family, none of this would have happened. Second, I want to thank those who have contributed significantly through their challenging ideas and by pushing me toward differing ways of developing the ideas. This group includes best friends Kevin and Amy, along with my idols Glen Johnson and Saul Young. For those moments when I was stuck and not able to accomplish anything at all, I was able to tap into the work of June Kuramoto for inspiration (I'm still waiting for my tix, June!) and into the powerfully creative abilities of my good friend Pepe. Finally, I must thank the editor and *the man* Sheck Cho for his understanding during the late submissions and for making this a much more pleasurable experience than I thought it would be. It has been great to work with him.

Contents

1

Limitations of Cost Accounting

The need to understand costs is a clear one. Organizations need to know what their costs are in order to determine and manage their profitability. To aid in determining their profitability, organizations need to understand what their total costs were, are, or are going to be over a given period of time. The difference between the revenue for that period and the costs incurred during the same period determines the profitability for the period. Thus, since costs normally are visible to an organization for historical periods to the present, profits and organizational performance easily can be determined. An organization might observe, for example, "We were profitable two years ago, increased our profits by 15 percent last year, and are on pace for a 10 percent increase this year." Understanding costs and the dynamics of costs yesterday and today helps managers make decisions so that they can effect current and future profits. Clearly, the better that costs and the impact of decisions on costs are understood, the greater the potential for more effective decision making. The effective management of costs is important for at least two reasons:

1. Effective management of costs can help improve profitability.
2. Effective management of costs can indicate management competence.

IMPROVING PROFITABILITY

Ultimately, decisions are made in for-profit organizations to drive profitability. While other salient factors help to determine the long-term viability of an organization, without profitable performance, long-term viability is not an option. In order to survive for the long run, an organization ultimately must be able to show that it can make more money from a product or service than it cost to make that product or service. The importance of understanding costs and managing costs to help manage and improve profitability can be categorized into four scenarios:

1. Organizations must be able to increase revenues at a consistent cost level.
2. Organizations must be able to reduce costs given consistent revenue levels.
3. Organizations must increase revenues at a rate faster than costs increase.
4. Organizations must decrease costs at a rate faster than revenues decrease.

The math in this situation is simple: Profits are equal to the difference between revenues and costs. Profits can be increased in only three ways. First, if the costs were to remain relatively constant for a period, revenues must be increased given the same level of costs. In other words, more output for a given input level must be achieved. This is the definition of productivity at a high level. Second, and similarly, if the revenues were to remain the same, reducing costs would have a positive impact on the profitability of the organization. This, too, would ultimately be considered an overall productivity increase since the organization is still getting a high level of output for a lower level of input. The final option is one to consider when the markets are more dynamic. If operating in an expanding market, the rate of increase of revenues must be greater than the rate of costs to ensure that profits continue to grow. If the market is getting smaller, the rate of revenue loss must be offset with cost-cutting measures that occur at a greater rate.

Increasing Revenues

In the first scenario, it is assumed that an organization is operating in a slowly expanding or a stagnant market. The adverb *slowly* is used

Exhibit 1.1   Increasing Revenues Through Increases in Productivity

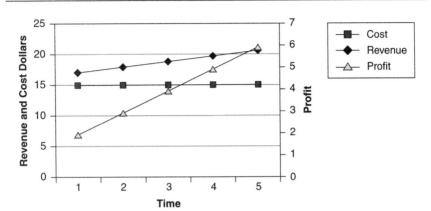

because costs must be managed more carefully in this environment versus a fast-growing market. An increase in costs should reflect an increase in capacity, which should ultimately increase revenues. However, with a market that is either stagnant or growing slowly, additional capacity does not offer much because the market limits sales. In this case, therefore, managers must try to keep costs from growing. They must look to maximize the output of existing resources while constraining cost growth so that additional revenues can be achieved without substantially increasing the organization's capacity. As shown in (Exhibit 1.1), this would be considered a traditional productivity increase as the organization is selling more (output) from the same resources (input).

Reducing Costs

In the second scenario, the focus is on reducing costs when the revenues are stagnant or slowly declining. The difference between this scenario and the first is that in a declining market, the focus is more on cost reduction while in an expanding market, cost maintenance or slight cost growth is the focus. In this case, the market might be somewhat stagnant and there is pressure to maintain or increase profits. When sales are limited, the only other option to maintain profitability is to reduce costs. As mentioned previously, this would be considered a productivity increase since the organization is getting the same output as before with less input. For more information regarding increasing profits by increasing efficiencies, see (Exhibit 1.2).

Exhibit 1.2   Increasing Profits by Increasing Efficiency

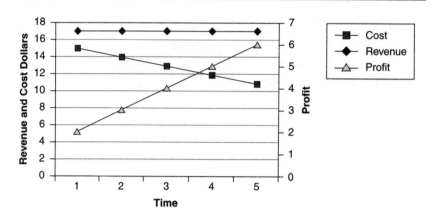

Rate of Revenue Increase

In the third scenario, two situations are actually involved. In the first situation, the organization might be operating in an expanding market. If a market is expanding and if the organization is capitalizing on the growth, revenues are going to increase. The question then becomes: How are costs being managed to ensure that profits increase? If costs are increasing at a rate greater than revenues, it is clear that the profits will be reduced, which may or may not be negative for the organization. If the costs are increasing for investment purposes, it may be positive depending on the outcome of the investments. If the investments fail and the organization is less profitable, the situation is clearly suboptimal. If, however, the investments succeed, the organization may be better off in the long run. The investments do not have to be purely financial investments. For example, if the organization is investing in its infrastructure, this may enable future growth or eliminate the opportunity to constrain future growth by ensuring that future capacity will be available. In the second situation, organizations might be looking at operational improvements. If the sales increase because of a cost increase, it is positive for the organization as long as the sales increase is at a rate greater than the cost increase (Exhibit 1.3).

Rate of Cost Decrease

The final case assumes a declining market or margins eroding at a reasonable to rapid pace. The objective is to ensure that costs are being reduced at a rate that is at least equal to and preferably greater

Exhibit 1.3   Effects of Managing Costs during Periods of Increasing
Revenues

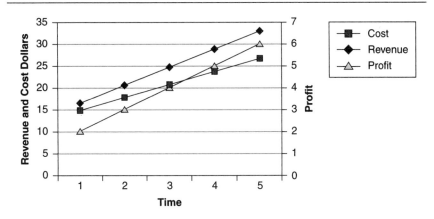

Exhibit 1.4   Minimizing Profit Loss in Declining Markets

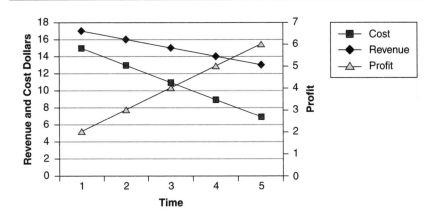

than the rate at which revenues are declining. Since there may be multiple dynamics involved in this situation, it is very important for managers to have the relevant information to make their decisions. In the case of a declining market, the assumption is that available capacity will increase due to a reduction in demand. Managers will need to know how much capacity is available and the cost of that capacity so that decisions can be made whether to reduce the capacity or to maintain it for future use. If the choice is to reduce capacity, the impact on cost, profit, and infrastructure must be understood so that managers can be sure that they are making the right decisions for financial and operational purposes (Exhibit 1.4).

MANAGEMENT COMPETENCE

Effective cost management can also indicate competent organizational management. This is especially important in an environment where organizations are often land-grabbing while trying to develop web-based and other strong technology-oriented businesses in areas such as biotechnology. Investors understand that in many cases there will be no revenues or that there will be no profits for long periods of time. The gamble is on the relevance of the idea and the competence of management to efficiently and effectively operationalize the idea. Relevance without competence, however, will not sustain a business for long. By showing competence in terms of how the business increases or decreases its capacity, management sends a message that should be interpreted by current and future investors that this management group has the knowledge and capability of achieving its vision and is therefore worthy of the investors' capital.

Because understanding the dynamics of costs is important, organizations spend a significant amount of time and money learning and using various techniques so that the dynamics of their cost can be understood. A number of techniques used in the past and today help organizations understand their cost dynamics. Many, if not all, of the major techniques are created on the basis of allocating costs to a unit of production in a manufacturing environment.

NEED TO ACCOUNT FOR COSTS

Assume that a large percentage of an organization's costs is created by the direct labor force. Assume, additionally, that these individuals were not paid by the hour but by the piece. This scenario describes many manufacturing companies at the turn of the century and earlier. If, for example, 90 percent of all costs were incurred by paying workers for the pieces they had produced and the material they had consumed, it is easy to see that direct labor, those involved directly with producing the goods, would be considered a varying cost. It costs the organization more to make the $n + 1$st unit than it does to make the nth unit. Therefore, in this scenario, the unit of production impacts a significant amount of the costs that the organization incurs.

What does the organization do with the other 10 percent of the costs? These costs typically do not vary directly, if at all, with the number of items being produced. Traditionally, the answer chosen was to allocate the cost by dividing the 10 percent of the costs by the number of units produced. If an organization were to allocate this 10 percent, it would place the unit of production into the center of its cost dynamics decision making. With the information now available, a unit cost can be determined.

Consider the following example. An organization spends $10.00 for every unit produced. This value includes labor and materials. It also has costs not associated with the production of its products of $100.00 for the period. The question is: How much will it cost for the organization to make X products? The computation for the example is very simple. If the direct cost for the organization is $10.00 for every unit produced, to determine the total direct cost, multiply the unit rate by the number of units produced. Thus, to produce 10 units, it would cost $100.00 because the organization would pay the workers for what they produced and the suppliers for what it bought. This is a linear relationship. The more that is produced, the more it costs by a constant amount neglecting some type of bonus structure (for example, if the worker makes 100 or more, the pay increases by $1.00 so that the total cost per unit is $11.00).

The costs that are not directly related, or the indirect costs, are a different story. The indirect costs are fixed, meaning they do not vary with production. However, organizations traditionally chose to include the indirect costs in the unit cost in order to absorb the impact of the cost. This is done through allocating. The idea is that each unit of production takes a portion of the indirect costs associated with running the business. The mathematics in this case are simple also. To determine an indirect cost per unit, divide the indirect costs by the number of units produced. If the indirect cost is fixed, dividing it by a number that increases (units produced) creates the effect of a reduction in the cost per unit. As more units are produced, the amount being absorbed is reduced (Exhibit 1.5).

To determine the total cost per unit, simply add the direct cost per unit to the indirect cost per unit (Exhibit 1.6). With this unit cost, many decisions can be made. First, by understanding how much a unit costs to make, pricing and production decisions are easier to make. For example, if it costs $15.00 to make one unit, the product can be sold at $16.00 to make a profit. Similarly, if the market price is $14.00 for the same unit, the organization may choose not to produce and sell the product. However, if more units are produced and

Exhibit 1.5   Indirect Labor/Unit as a Function of Units Produced

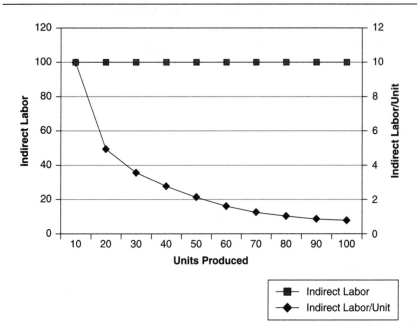

the unit cost of production is reduced to, say, $13.00, the market price of $14.00 may now become attractive.

Clearly, this technique of allocating costs has holes. To spread the indirect costs evenly across products may not be appropriate. What if, for instance, the number of units produced is comprised of multiple products? What if the indirect resources spend unequal amounts of time on the different products? Should all products absorb the same amount of the indirect costs? The answer at the time was generally yes. Remember that at the time, indirect labor costs were such a small amount of the total costs that the amount absorbed and the differences between what might be considered right or wrong were negligible. In other words, the amount was too small to be concerned about.

Over time, the concept of accounting became more complicated for various reasons, including the following:

1. Hourly rates for employees were introduced.
2. Industrial engineering standards impacted the perception of what costs should be.

Exhibit 1.6   Total Cost Per Unit Decreases with Increased Production

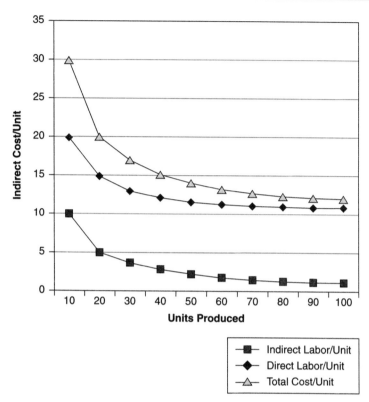

Hourly Rates

The introduction of hourly rates creates a different dynamic in terms of managing costs. Recall before the introduction of hourly wages, a worker was paid on output. Assume that workers who made 10 parts would be paid $100.00. If they made 10 parts in 40 hours, they would be paid the equivalent of $2.50/hour. If two parts per day were an expected output, the organization could choose to pay the employee $20.00/day for an anticipated eight-hour workday. Although the math and the accounting might be simpler for the organization and hourly payments may be more attractive in terms of hiring and maintaining employees, this change made the concept of accounting for costs more complicated. With hourly wages no longer directly tied to the cost of producing a unit, they also had to be allocated. Whenever a cost is spread across entities by dividing,

Exhibit 1.7   Comparing Hourly Cost/Unit to Piecework Cost/Unit

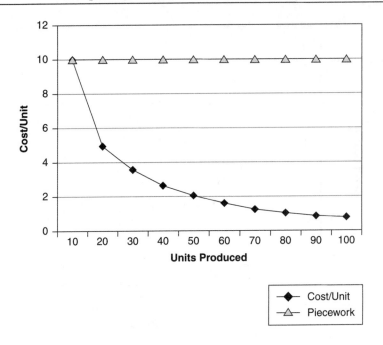

the assumption is that each item is getting an equal share of the amount being spread. So, if the employee made 20 parts in 40 hours rather than the 10 that was expected, the cost of production *had* to go down. Why? Because each unit must now absorb a portion of the direct labor costs as well, and the larger the number of units produced, the smaller the cost amount allocated to each unit. The result is that the direct labor cost per unit goes down when more is produced (Exhibit 1.7). The assumption remained, therefore, that direct labor was a variable cost; the more that a person produced, the lower the unit cost.

Industrial Engineering

Industrial engineering introduced another approach: the time standard.[1] Time standards are used as a basis to determine the amount of time that it should take to make a product. Going back to the worker discussed previously, it may have been determined that, on average, the employee can make two units per day, or one unit every four hours. This information can be used for multiple reasons. Standards can be used:

- to determine a standard cost to produce
- to determine and improve manufacturing efficiency and productivity

Standard Cost

In practice, the standard cost is a simple concept. It is the cost that the organization incurs to make an item if production is operating and consuming materials at a standard rate. For example, if an employee who makes $20.00 per day makes two units each day, the math suggests that it costs $10.00 per unit in direct labor cost at standard (Equation 1.1). In general, the product of the time standard and the labor rate, as seen in Equation 1.2, determines the standard labor cost per unit. This information is used as a basis for understanding operational performance and to get a quick feel of what a product does cost or should cost.

$$\frac{8 \text{ Hours}}{2 \text{ Units}} \times \frac{\$20.00}{8 \text{ Hours Direct Labor}} = \frac{\$10.00}{\text{Unit}} \qquad (1.1)$$

$$\text{Labor Standard } (^{\text{Hours}}\!/_{\text{Unit}}) \times \text{Labor Cost } (^{\$}\!/_{\text{Hour}}) = \\ \text{Standard Labor Cost } (^{\$}\!/_{\text{Unit}}) \qquad (1.2)$$

Efficiency and Productivity

Due to variations that can result from multiple sources, workers often do not operate exactly at standard. At times they might be a little slower than the standard, and at other times they might be faster. Understanding the actual rate of production can be used to determine an actual cost, which, under the circumstances described previously, is different than the standard cost (Equation 1.3). Since it is assumed that direct labor varies, it is important to understand the impact of the change in production rate, or the variance between what was expected and what actually happened. This variance in cost is simply the difference between the standard cost and the actual cost (Equation 1.4). If the actual cost is less than the standard cost, there is a favorable variance; if it is less, there is an unfavorable variance. So, if the employee only makes 1.5 units per day, each unit must absorb more of the fixed cost of the labor. The actual unit cost in this case goes up to $13.33 per unit, leading to an unfavorable variance of $3.33. If the output goes up to four units, the cost goes down to $5.00 per unit, leading to a favorable variance of $5.00. The more a worker positively exceeds the standard, the lower the actual cost and the higher the favorable variance (Exhibit 1.8).

$$\text{Actual Labor Rate } (^{\text{Hours}}\!/_{\text{Unit}}) \times \text{Labor Cost } (^{\$}\!/_{\text{Hour}}) =$$
$$\text{Actual Labor Cost } (^{\$}\!/_{\text{Unit}}) \qquad (1.3)$$

$$\text{Cost Variance} = \text{Standard Cost} - \text{Actual Cost} \qquad (1.4)$$

If an organization finds that it consistently has unfavorable variances, the standards may be difficult for the organization to meet. By not meeting the standard, the products are considered more expen-

Exhibit 1.8   Production Rates and the Impact on Actual Cost and Cost Variance

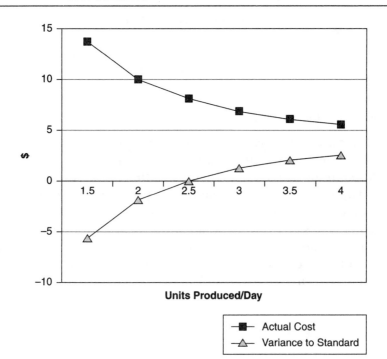

sive to make than expected from a unit cost perspective. In this case, the options are basically to improve operations to help make up for the variance in other ways, to find ways for the operators to operate more quickly, or to change the standard. In other situations, the standards may be too aggressive, in which case the engineers and the workers would collaborate to lower the value for expected output. The result would be products with a higher unit cost, but that cost would be considered a more reasonable number from cost and people management perspectives.

If there were always favorable variances, the standards might not be aggressive enough. Constantly beating the standard would suggest that meeting the standard might be too *easy* for the operation and that a more reasonable target rate should be chosen. By increasing the standard operating rate, the product cost per unit would go down, leading to products that are believed to be less expensive to make.

IMPACT OF STANDARD COSTING ON OPERATIONS

Understanding cost behavior and cost dynamics from the standard-cost perspective made cost management both more manageable and less manageable. It also created certain behavior in the organization that was both more desirable and less desirable.

More Manageable

From the perspective of understanding how outputs (production) and inputs (labor) interact, standard-costing techniques started to enable discussions regarding efficiency and productivity and their implied impact on the bottom line. For example, managers began to financially understand, whether correctly or not, that increased productivity and efficiency can impact the bottom line of the organization. The belief, for instance, was that increased efficiency and increased productivity could reduce costs, which would lead to positive bottom-line results. This drove certain behavior, such as trying to focus on areas to manage and reduce costs in order to increase profits. Motion and time study, for example, is an exercise to drive down costs based on standards. By viewing how an operation is performed and by identifying improvements, operations standards could be improved, leading to lower standard costs for products.

Less Manageable

Costs from this perspective also become less manageable for multiple reasons:

- In reality, a large portion of total costs are being allocated arbitrarily.
- Variance analysis adds to the complexity of cost management.
- Organizations begin to lose control and visibility of their cost drivers.
- Organizations are beginning to understand that cost dynamics exist but are learning the wrong aspects of cost dynamics.

Arbitrary Allocations

As discussed previously, standard-costing techniques often allocate costs based on standards. These standards might not reflect reality if improperly determined, if not updated to reflect the current state of operations, or if the standards are not consistent with what creates the costs being allocated. Standards might be improperly determined, for instance, if improper assumptions were made regarding the capabilities of the operations. If standards were determined in a controlled setting where the assumptions leading to the control do not reflect the reality of the operation, the standards are likely to be incorrect. For example, in a controlled setting, all incoming materials might be perfectly to specification, whereas in a real situation, the materials might include defects, which can impact the number of good parts coming out of the operation.

In addition, an organization's standards are often found to be outdated. Organizations often go through an extensive process to determine standards and then will assume improvements from anecdotal information, leaving others to question the relevance of the standards. One organization determined its standards a number of years in the past and measured performance increases by analyzing year-to-year variances and job-to-job variances. Improvements were determined based on the value of the variance vis-à-vis previous jobs. Improvements, therefore, were discussed in terms of whether an unfavorable variance was reduced or whether a favorable variance had increased using standards often many years old as the basis.

Finally, one of the biggest problems associated with standard costing is the fact that costs are being allocated using values that may have nothing to do with why the costs were incurred in the first place. Assume, for instance, that an organization makes two products, A and B. Although A and B take the exact same amount of direct labor to produce, because B is a custom product, 90 percent of the time of the indirect labor force is focused on supporting the needs of B. If allocation is performed using direct labor hours, as is the case using standard-costing techniques, the indirect labor is spread evenly across the products. This hides the fact that much of the activities of the indirect labor is being driven by the needs associated with supporting B. Standard costing would suggest, in this case, that the costs would be the same for both products; logic would suggest that B should cost more because it creates the majority of the costs. This is not as much of a problem when only 10 percent or so of an organization's costs are being allocated. However, many organizations today find that a significant percentage and often a clear majority of its costs are being allocated, inferring that unit costs are very much out of alignment with real costs.

Variance Analysis

The concept of a variance analysis that is driven by standard labor or operating hours is fairly complicated and very time consuming. First, the conditions leading to the variance in the first place have often passed, which reduces the potential to identify meaningful operation attributes. For example, if the organization identifies a favorable variance, can it also identify the specific circumstances that led to the variance? Can it identify what may have led to an unfavorable variance to the extent that process changes can be made? Second, the relevance of the analysis must be checked. If a significant amount of costs are being allocated using standards, slight variations in actual versus standards may have a very large implication in unit cost; in the overall scheme of things in a profit-focused environment, however, the slight difference does not matter at all.

Losing Control and Visibility of Cost Drivers

With the focus being on standards, the issue becomes how an organization determines why fixed costs exist in the first place. In the

earlier example where product B requires 90 percent of the resources, the organization loses visibility to this fact when focusing
on standards. Organizations need to be able to understand why
they incur costs without the ambiguity created by standard-costing
techniques.

Learning the Wrong Aspects of Cost Dynamics

With documented techniques for accounting for costs, organizations
can begin to understand the dynamics of costs—how and why they
change. However, they often are learning the wrong dynamics. Fixed
costs, for example, may not change with changes in production
amounts, yet these systems often suggest that they do. From this perspective, organizations begin to focus on the dynamics of a unit of
production rather than the dynamics of the bottom line. As described in the next section, unit cost dynamics and bottom-line cost
dynamics are not the same.

Desirable Behavior

Much of the desirable behavior that resulted from standard costing
centered on the idea of making costs and cost improvement opportunities salient in the minds of those making decisions. Along
with motion and time study and other techniques, standard costing
focused improvements on saving time and reducing waste in the
operations. For the most part, this is positive for the organization
as long as the efforts are appropriately focused. Increasing speed to
reduce unit cost is an example of one area of focus for some organizations. The idea of optimization could now be applied to
product mix, procurement, and setup which led to techniques and
equations that supposedly reduced costs or at least sought to *optimize costs*.[2] Finally, ways to measure and to provide incentives for
workers was now available. If organizations met or favorably ex-
ceeded standards, they were rewarded because meeting or exceed-
ing standards meant that all costs were absorbed at least as expected and sometimes more favorably.

Undesirable Behavior

The undesirable behavior driven by standard-costing techniques is
centered on the following two topics:

1. Belief that focusing on unit costs and on production is the correct way to manage cost dynamics
2. Belief that unit cost reduction leads to profit enhancement

Unit Costs and Production as Focus of Cost Dynamics

Because of the ease of documenting cost per unit changes, organizations began to place production and the unit cost at the forefront of their thinking. If costs were allocated based on standard labor hours, the more the production time reduced or the overall output increased, the lower the cost per unit. Since the cost per unit was a controllable portion of the unit margin (revenue/unit − cost/unit), organizations began to focus on reducing costs through decisions in production.

The results of such thinking were disastrous. First, organizations began to focus on efficiency, utilization, and economy-of-scale measures in ways that were not good for manufacturing. For example, the efficiency and utilization measures caused production managers to make sure that the machines and the workers were operating as close to 100 percent of the time as possible. While it seems that this would be beneficial to organizations, in a great majority of the measures that were used to drive production, demand was not taken into account. As a result, organizations often produced much more than demand required so that costs were reduced. Second, the organizations began to operate assuming that large batches were actually cheaper to process. Organizations began to practice combining batches that had similar setups to reduce the downtime of the operation and, therefore, the cost of the operation. This was often done without considering the downstream effects of the action. In one factory, for instance, an operator with plenty of capacity took it upon himself to combine batches even though the production schedulers did not recommend the practice. This practice ultimately was praised by managers and proudly was discussed as an example of an empowered workforce. The problem with the practice was that it created havoc in their downstream heat-treat operations. Materials with differing heat-treat requirements arrived into the queue at inopportune times, leading to poor efficiency at the limited-capacity *heat-treat* operation. Third, most organizations began to break processes up into their constitutive components, analyzed the components, optimized the components individually, and assumed that when the process was fully operational, the overall process was optimized. As discussed by many experts such as Eli Goldratt, this practice actually suboptimizes the overall operations, as was seen in the heat-treat example discussed previously.[3]

Profit Enhancement through Unit Cost Reduction

The other major undesired behavior is that profit enhancement was assumed to occur through increasing unit margins. This is incorrect for two reasons:

1. Even though the cost per unit goes down, the bottom-line costs may not change, leading organizations to believe that they are better off than they actually are.
2. To assume that changes in unit cost reduction through allocation with labor standards as drivers reduces overall costs is inaccurate.

Margin Enhancement as Profit Enhancement

The assumption that margin enhancement equals profit enhancement is simple but also incorrect. Since unit margin is equal to the difference between unit revenue and unit cost, it is assumed that as the unit cost goes down, the profit per unit goes up. Conceptually, this is true; however, as unit costs go down, total costs do not always go down (see, for example, Exhibits 1.5 and 1.7). The expenses of the organization determine the cost component of profit, and as seen in the aforementioned examples, the expenses incurred do not go down as production increases. In each case, although the amount of money that the organization spends is the same, the perception might be that the organization is making money by doing more. However, because the focus is on the unit cost, efforts to reduce this cost often lead to overproduction and overall wasteful behavior.

Reducing Costs by Reducing Standards

When using standard-costing techniques, costs are allocated based on standard labor hours. In the earliest and simpler forms of allocation, this allocation would include indirect labor. So, as the standard was decreased, the amount of indirect labor absorbed by each unit was reduced, leading to a lower unit cost. As time progressed and as more and more allocable costs were independent of the number of units produced or the time required for each unit, standards often still drove the cost allocation process.

ACTIVITY-BASED COSTING

Although standard costing offered improvements over what was available previously, a number of serious issues associated with its use remained. There were fundamental questions that organizations needed to be able to answer with their costing system. Among the questions were the following:

- What are the true costs of producing certain products?
- What are the true costs of serving customers?
- What is the cause of the significant amount of indirect labor that exists?

Although these questions are very important to the decision making process and operation of an organization, they are unanswerable, at best, by standard costing. If the question is unanswered or made based on anecdotal information, it might be better than being led down a wrong path by the precision of the standard-costing system. It supports the application of the cliché: *It is better to be approximately right than precisely wrong.*

Activity-based costing (ABC) was created to provide more meaningful allocation of costs. It is still an allocation technique, but the costs are allocated using what are considered to be more relevant drivers or bases for allocation. Thus, using the earlier example with the two products, A and B, B would get 90 percent of the indirect labor costs using ABC. This allocation process suggests that ABC is more relevant, leading to a better representation of costs and their dynamics.

How ABC Works

Activity-based costing focuses on identifying the large cost drivers associated with a decision to be made or a process being analyzed. The allocation, then, is based on that which drives the costs that affect the decision. The following examples explain how ABC answers the questions posed previously.

What Are the True Costs?

Assume again that there are two products, A and B, that have the same production requirements. The activities that the indirect labor force undertakes to support B require 90 percent of its time. If there were $10,000.00 in indirect labor to be allocated, product B would get $9,000.00. The $9,000.00 would then be allocated evenly to each B that is produced. If there were 1,000 units of both A and B produced, each unit of A would receive $1.00 while each unit of B would receive $9.00. This is compared to each unit receiving $5.00. With this information, it is believed that organizations can more effectively price the products to ensure that they achieve the right margin.

What Are the Costs of Serving Customers?

Although many techniques exist to determine the cost of serving certain customers, an organization would simply use the same technique employed to determine "true" costs. For example, if the organization spent 90 percent of its customer service efforts on one client, then 90 percent of the pool of costs could somehow be allocated to the products purchased by that client. The organization could then decide how to deal with the excessive costs of serving that customer, including trying to increase the price of the products sold to this customer or choosing not to serve the customer at all.

What Is Driving the Costs That Exist?

The concept of activity-based management is really an extension of ABC without the cost information being allocated. Simply, an organization can look at the activities associated with a pool of labor to help determine whether the resources are being used efficiently and effectively. For example, if, after performing an analysis, the organization finds that 40 percent of its time is not being effectively utilized, management decisions can be made either to reduce the cost or to more effectively utilize the resources.

Good Idea or Not?

In general, what ABC attempts to achieve may be beneficial to the organization. The desire is to allocate based on relevant drivers.

However, in the limit, ABC is still an allocation technique and still has significant limitations.

- As with standard costing, the cost-per-unit focus provides misinformation regarding bottom-line cost dynamics. Once the costs have been allocated using more relevant drivers, there is still the issue of dividing the total cost pool by the number of units produced, suggesting that costs go down even though they may be fixed.

- How does an organization handle varying activities? If the organization spends 90 percent of its time on an activity on Monday, 50 percent on Tuesday, and 10 percent on Wednesday, do the costs of the products to which the pool is being allocated on those days change? Are the products more expensive on Monday than on Wednesday? Does the organization use an average? If it uses an average, is it weighted? How many weighting options exist? Does the organization use the average if there is a large standard deviation?

- How does an organization handle inefficient operations? What if only 80 percent of the time is allocable? What happens to the other 20 percent? Is the decision of what to do with the 20 percent arbitrary?

- ABC is another allocation methodology with arbitrary cost drivers. Two individuals can assess the same situation in different ways and determine different costs per unit. Although the logic appears to be in place and although the concept attempts to answer many of the right questions, the results of an ABC analysis and the use of these results are still highly questionable.

NEED FOR NONALLOCATION COST MANAGEMENT

It is apparent that ABC is still not enough, and the problems center on the allocation of costs. Allocation exists for the purpose of understanding operations and cost dynamics. However, allocation-based cost management systems fail to provide this information because they create situations that do not exist. As will be shown in Chapter 2, for example, under no circumstance can costs go down as a result of doing more. By dividing two numbers, an illusion of cost dynamics is created, which suggests that the more a person does, the cheaper it is to do it. The bottom line, however, tells a different story, and only the bottom line determines profitability.

Instead, a cost management system is needed where there is no allocation and yet information is provided that is at least as important as organizations believe they are getting from their existing cost management systems.

Endnotes

[1] Although material standards exist and are used in ways similar to labor standards, their use adds nothing to the discussion and will therefore not be considered further.

[2] One must question whether costs can be optimized at all. Does it mean maximize costs? If it means minimize costs, then not operating the business is the lowest cost solution. One optimizes profits by maximizing the difference between revenues and costs.

[3] See, for example, Eliyahu M. Goldratt and Jeff Cox, *The Goal: A Process of Ongoing Improvement,* 2nd ed. (Croton-on-Hudson, NY: North River Press, 1992).

2

What Is Explicit Cost Dynamics?

Explicit cost dynamics (ECD) is a new framework for understanding and managing costs. As a management tool, ECD can be described as a nonallocation-based cost management system that aids management in making forward-thinking cost and profit decisions from both tactical and strategic perspectives. The framework uses the bottom line as a basis for developing the concepts and measures used, because the bottom line is used by most businesses and stockholders to assess the financial and operational performance of a company. Current allocation-based cost management systems do not provide an adequate, direct bottom-line correlation between what they propose in use and what actually happens to the bottom line. Examples will typically involve decisions associated with time savings and economies of scale but also include misunderstandings created when an organization arbitrarily allocates costs to something independent of what created the cost. With that being the case, it is useful for managers to have a cost management system that ensures they make decisions that tie directly to the bottom line.

WHAT DOES THE NAME *EXPLICIT COST DYNAMICS* MEAN?

The name *explicit cost dynamics* was selected to reduce ambiguity in terms of what the framework is, what it explains, and where the emphasis is placed. Because each term is quite important in defining ECD, this section focuses on explaining each term in the context of the framework. Before defining each term, however, a context must be created that is of fundamental importance. ECD is created from and focuses on the bottom line of a company's financials. The argument for ECD is not centered on the importance of the bottom line. Rather, the bottom line is the source of least ambiguity in terms of providing cost information for management purposes.

Bottom-Line Impact

Companies manage and control costs due to the presumed impact of the actions on the bottom line. After all, if the bottom line is not affected, why manage costs? ECD focuses on the concept of a bottom-line impact (BLI). When an organization makes a decision in support of new technologies, for example, it should know, to a high level of detail and confidence, what the cost of the technology will be and what bottom-line impact implementing the technology will have. Likewise, to determine how best to utilize resources, predictable bottom-line behavior will help managers ensure optimal operations. A differentiating factor between ECD and other cost systems is that ECD ensures, in proper application, that BLIs are both known and predictable. Other cost systems often find cost improvements when, in fact, there might not be any cost improvements at all. For example, when increasing the productivity of a design engineer, where are the cost improvements? While a cost-benefit analysis might try to assume some cost savings based on the salary of the engineer, these savings do not exist. The engineer's capacity might have been freed by a technology or process change, but unless someone is released from the organization as a result of the action or the company reduces the salary of the engineer, costs will remain the same. Only when there is a conscious effort to reduce the money that the company is spending will there be a BLI.

Explicit

The term *explicit* refers to the actual flow of money into and away from a company. The emphasis on explicit money flow results from complications that arise if implicit flows, or money that does not really exist, are considered. Focusing on implicit flows gives companies a false view of their true cost dynamics. Explicit dollar flows are highlighted in this framework because they, alone, are used to determine bottom-line profitability. For example, if a manager must transfer money from his or her budget to the budget of another manager, there is no direct BLI created by this transaction. Without an impact on the bottom line, there is no direct impact on the profitability of the company resulting from the decision. If, however, this manager purchases the same service from an outside vendor, money leaves the company, leading to an action with a BLI.

Cost

The term *cost* refers to money leaving the company. The decision to use the term *cost* is a difficult one because most people believe that they already know what a cost is. A traditional definition of costs that might be considered generally understood is: *Costs measure the dollar value of any inputs used over any period to produce an item.*[1] This type of definition leads to many questions. What is an input? What is an item? Does an item only represent something tangible such as a widget? What about costs that do not produce an item? Since human resources (HR) does not produce an item, are the activities of this department costs? Are the people hired by HR items? What if the firm does not make items? Do services count? Information? How does an organization determine at what rate costs measure inputs? Obviously, such a definition creates immediate questions that leave any dialogue about costs open to interpretation. One person has an interpretation of what a cost is that might be somewhat different from another person's definition, which might be completely different from a third person's definition. To top it off, there is still no assurance that a BLI will occur as a result of managing to this definition.

Because of the ambiguity associated with this definition of a cost, ECD uses a different definition. For the purposes of ECD, *costs measure the actual flow of money from a company over a period resulting from being in business and operating the business.* There must be a BLI for something to be considered a cost. Companies incur costs every day that are not associated with an item or, to expand the definition provided, a service. Is subsidized parking for accountants not a cost because it is not an input to produce an item? It is a cost if the company has to pay someone or a separate entity for the parking.

Dynamics

Dynamics refers to how something changes. The dynamics of costs, as will be shown throughout this book, are not well understood. Existing cost management systems tend to obscure the dynamics of costs. Cost functions are monotonically increasing functions. What does this mean? A function whose dependent variable (total cost or sales) increases as the independent variable (units or sales transactions) increases is said to be a monotonically increasing function. The more an organization ships, the greater its shipping costs; it cannot ship more and have the bottom-line cost go down. The organization can identify the dynamics of shipping charges by plotting a curve or creating a chart. Once this information is available to the right individuals, they will begin to understand the dynamics behind shipping costs.

Cost dynamics usually ties costs to time, actions, or items. If a company pays someone by the hour, the more the person works, the greater is the cost to pay that person. An eight-hour day costs more than a five-hour day; time is money in this case. Not all costs are time dependent to the same degree. For example, if a company pays someone $100.00 per day, a five-hour day costs the same as an eight-hour day. The BLI is the same inside of one day. Although the potential for what can be accomplished might be less in a five-hour day than it is for an eight-hour day, that, in and of itself, does not cause an increase in cost. In this case, time is not really money. For someone paid on an hourly basis, as the number of hours increases, the cost to the organization increases. For someone paid on a daily basis, costs only increase when the number of days worked increases. This distinction is very important when managing costs. Costs can also be a function of an activity. For example, the more times the activity of shipping is performed, the greater the shipping costs. In this case, shipping costs are independent of time but are, nonetheless, monotonically increasing cost functions with the independent variable being the number of shipments and the independent variable being the bottom-line shipping costs. Finally, in terms of purchasing, the more items purchased, the greater the purchasing cost.

Fundamentals of ECD

Although more detail follows in Chapter 5, it makes sense to discuss the fundamentals of ECD now. Actual money flow into and out of a company is the basis for ECD. Identifying the flow of money into and out of the company is what defines the flow as *explicit*. Every measure has a direct tie to the bottom line, because these flows are how the bottom line is defined from a cost management perspective. With every decision made using the ECD framework, an organization will be able to identify immediately what impact the resulting action will make on the bottom line and cash flow. No allocation-based costing system will do that in all cases. Using activity-based costing (ABC), for instance, a manager might assume that changing how a department allocates its resources to a product might lead to savings. According to ABC, if engineers spend 70 percent of their time on one product and 30 percent on another, changing this ratio would have an impact on the cost of the products; that is, the product that has a reduced amount of the engineers' time actually has a reduction in cost. This, however, is not true. The organization might be able to increase the price if the extra time spent by the engineers is represented as more value in the product. However, no matter how employees divide their time, if their pay does not change, the bottom-line cost remains the same. If the activities associated with producing the product stay the same, the bottom-line cost stays the same. The manager may counter with, "But the cost per piece will go down." Such a comment begs the response: "What sense does it make that the cost per piece goes down, but the bottom-line costs remain the same?"

NONALLOCATION COST MANAGEMENT

The math associated with costs should be easy to understand. How much did it cost to ship that product? $1,000.00. How much did the organization pay in labor costs last month? $100,000.00. These scenarios are easy to address, identify, and understand. Every time the company spends money on something, that transaction is identifiable. The costs are known quantities with no ambiguity. Where companies get into trouble is when questions based on the allocation of costs are involved. How much does it cost to make this widget? Well, it depends. Using cost method A, each one costs $12.50. Using cost method B with a more efficient allocation basis, it costs $14.82. If all costs and activities remain the same, why does the cost to make the item change? Although labor, material costs, and bottom-line costs are the same, different costing methods lead to different unit costs. Which cost is right? Is either correct? Companies spend millions of dollars on trying to figure out whether method B is better than A and on implementing what they believe is the best allocation method. When the allocation basis is changeable, how does the company know that method B is better than method A? Is it because method B is *less arbitrary?* How is *less arbitrary* measured? What is the BLI created by the gap?

There should be a duality associated with cost management. *Duality* is a term used in physics that is applicable in this environment. The concept of duality suggests that regardless of the method used to arrive at a solution, the same solution should always be obtained. All methods used should lead to the same answer. Even if two people have different hypotheses about the same concept, verification of these hypotheses should lead to the same solution if the hypotheses are observing the same phenomenon. For example, hypotheses regarding acceleration due to gravity should all indicate that acceleration due to gravity is approximately 32.2 feet per second per second at sea level. There is one acceleration rate—32.2 feet per second per second. Regardless of the source of this acceleration, the effect is the same—32.2 feet per second per second. A hypothesis suggesting that acceleration due to gravity were 45.3 feet per second per second using one technique but 12.9 using another technique would be questioned. There would be something fundamentally wrong with this scenario.

If there were one true unit cost, all methods should converge on this one unit cost, regardless of the technique used. However, with the exact same inputs, costing systems can determine different unit costs. If there were a product cost, why would all methods not converge on this one cost? The question would then not be what the cost is; rather, the question should be how the company arrives at the cost. For example, one method might be twice as fast because some steps were left out, or data using one technique are easier to find and maintain than with the other. What sense does it make that accountants, managers, and organizations argue and spend millions of dollars for a process and, in some cases, supporting software that has absolutely no hope of giving them a meaningful answer?

Costs as Functions

Cost management should be based on functions that provide predictable and repeatable numbers. A function is a mathematical process that determines an answer (output) when numbers are placed into it (input). When numbers are placed into a function, one answer and only one answer comes out—this is how costs should work. Costs are not random variables that should change even if all of the conditions are the same. There should be no solution range of answers for costs, and there should be no cost-strange attractors that accurately predict where a cost might be given any set of circumstances. Cost equations and measures should be based on functions where values are placed into the function and one number comes out. Place numbers into the cost function, and out comes a unit cost. This is the same idea as the function machine used to teach functions in math: the numbers go into the machine on the top, and out pops the one and only answer on the side. 4 + 4 + 4 is equal to 12, which is always equal to 4 × 3. Regardless of the technique used, the answer remains the same. For example, multiplication might be faster than addition, and that is okay. Imagine the confusion if different techniques led to different answers: *The product of three and four is twelve and thirteen,* or *3 × 4 is 12 while 4 + 4 + 4 is 13.* No, it does not work this way. The product of three and four has been, is, and always will be twelve. Why do we allow costs to defy natural and simple mathematics?

Explicit cost dynamics eliminates the aforementioned problems with allocation-based systems. ECD explains the concept of cost flows, explains why allocations of costs lead to confusion, and identifies cost types and new measures that ensure bottom-line results of cost management decisions.

Cost Flows

Cost flows have linear behavior. Cost functions are monotonically increasing functions. If it costs $13.50 to send a package, then sending four packages costs $54.00. It cannot cost less to ship the $n + 1$st package than it does to ship the nth package. If a worker is paid $100.00 per day, working another day costs the company $100.00. Even if the extra day is overtime, the same rules apply. It simply costs more to do more. The linear relationship is found in Equation 2.1.

$$\text{Total Cost} = \text{Unit Rate} \times \text{Quantity Used} \qquad (2.1)$$

The unit rate is a ratio that represents the cost of one unit of the item or service being purchased. For example, a company might charge 10 cents per minute for long-distance telephone calls. In this case, the unit is one minute of long-distance service and the unit rate is the rate at which the company charges for one or several of the units (10 cents per minute). The unit rate is not always based on time, however. It might be based on actions. If a shipping company charges $20.00 per shipment, the unit rate is $20.00/shipment and the unit would be one shipment. The unit rate might also involve items. The unit rate for example might be $0.33 per first-class stamp. The unit in this case is one stamp. Thus, the unit rate will have either a time component ($ ÷ time), an action component ($ ÷ action), or an item component ($ ÷ item).

The unit rate determines the rate of increase of the cost curve. For example, assume that an employee makes $8.00 *per* hour (money ÷ time). As the employee works more, the amount paid to that person increases by the hourly rate (Exhibit 2.1). However, if the person works overtime, the unit rate for each hour of overtime is higher ($12,000 assuming time-and-a-half pay). In Exhibit 2.2, the relationship between costs and hours worked is linear throughout all time worked. The only difference is that the slope, or rate of increase of the total cost curve, increases because of the increased hourly rate from overtime. In this exhibit, it is assumed that the employee will now get $12.00 for each hour worked over eight. Although the rate of cost increase is greater for the time worked over eight hours, the

Exhibit 2.1   Hourly Labor Costs Increase Over Time

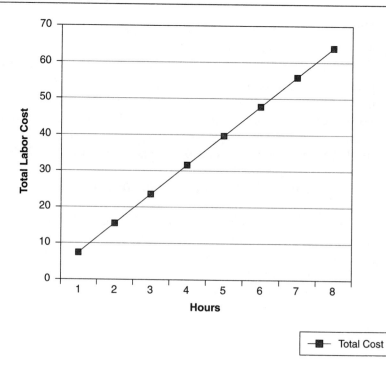

Exhibit 2.2 Hourly Labor Costs with Overtime

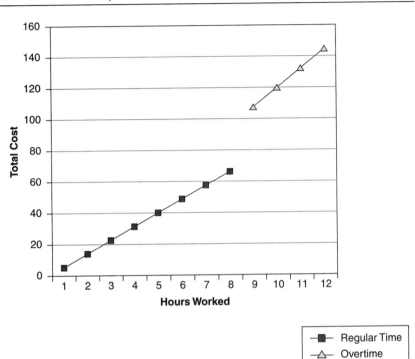

relationship is still linear. One more hour worked means another $12.00 paid rather than another $8.00.

The same is true for other types of costs. The total item costs for one more widget is determined by the unit rate for widgets and the number of widget components purchased. In the case of volume discounts, the relationship is linear; unlike overtime, however, the slope might increase at a slower rate rather than increase with increased occurrence to reflect the discounts (Exhibit 2.3). Assume that the company selling the items in this case sells them for $5.00 each for all units up to and including 50. The price per unit drops to $3.00 per unit for all units above 50. Therefore, the price for 65 units may be determined by calculating the price for 50 units at $5.00/unit and adding it to the additional 15 units priced at $3.00. The total price would be $295.00 (50 × $5.00 + 15 × $3.00). Once the discount range is reached, the unit rate is reduced from $5.00 to $3.00. This is why the slope of the cost

Exhibit 2.3   Impact of Volume Discounts on the Cost Curve

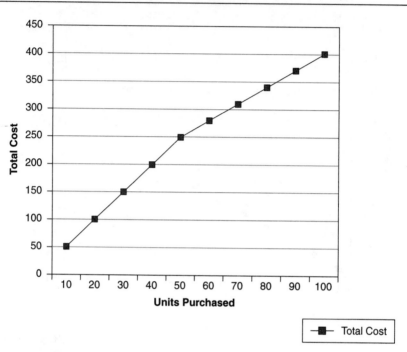

curve has changed. Nonetheless, the total cost still increases when buying more units.

Allocating Complicates Cost Management

Why introduce a nonallocation cost management system? Because the allocation of costs confuses people by doing two things. First, allocation creates a misunderstanding of how costs are incurred and how they behave. Second, because of the first issue, managers become thoroughly confused about how to manage costs in their organizations. Consider an example with an employee making $8.00 per hour.

Assume that the standard for this employee is 10 units of production per hour. At $8.00 for each hour worked, allocating labor costs leads to a desired unit cost of $0.80. Also assume a material cost of $0.50 per unit. Using a traditional approach, a unit cost of $1.30 might have been assumed. Exhibit 2.4 shows that if this person slacks off and decreases output to 9 units per hour, the labor cost increases to $0.89, which leads to a unit cost of $1.39. If the out-

Exhibit 2.4 Increasing Efficiency Is Assumed to Reduce Unit Cost

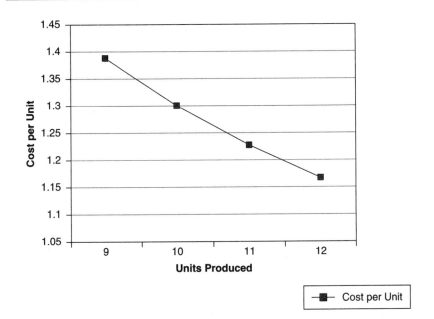

put increases to 12 units, the unit cost drops to $1.17. This probably makes sense to you; however, consider the following. First, labor costs remain the same in each scenario. The length of time and the labor rate remains the same. Second, material costs have increased with increased efficiency (more units require more materials). If labor is the same and if material costs have increased, how can it be cheaper to make more? Now, the more important questions. Why does it make sense that if bottom-line costs have increased, costs have gone down? If you had to make the decision, to which model would you manage? The model based on the bottom line suggests that the more a worker makes, the more costly it is to the company. The model based on allocation suggests that the more a worker makes, the less costly it is.

This confusion often can be found with purchasing goods at larger quantities. Referring to the example in which volume discounts were provided for units purchased above unit 50, if a unit purchase price were determined, it would appear that the more a person buys, the cheaper each unit becomes (Exhibit 2.5). Clearly, if a cost per unit were calculated, this value would be declining with increasing volume. For each unit above the 50th, the lower unit cost of these

Exhibit 2.5   Volume Discount Impact on Unit Cost

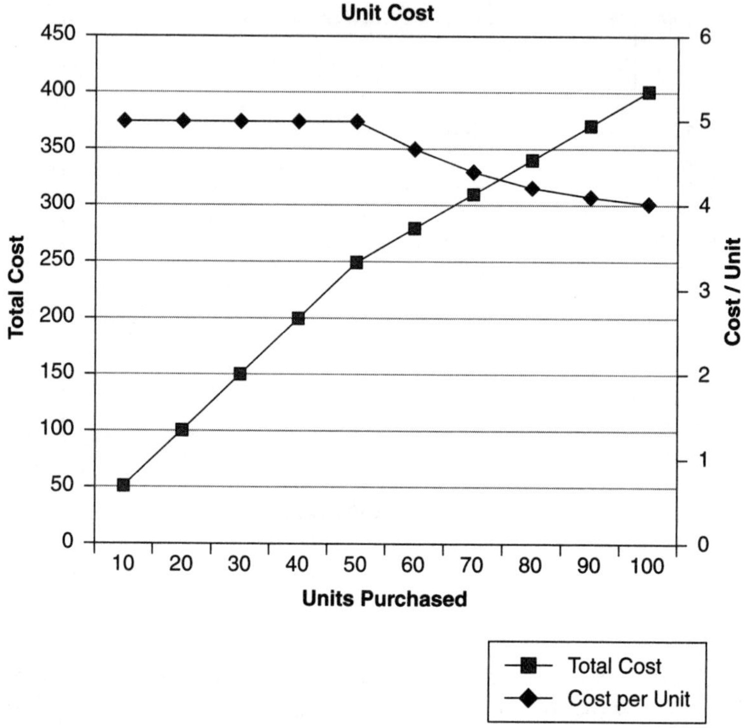

items will cause the average cost, which would determine the price per unit, to be lower, although the price per unit is lower, it is still more costly to buy more items (Exhibit 2.6). The dilemma resurfaces. Buy more because it is cheaper, or buy fewer because it is cheaper?

This dilemma largely has lead to the development of ECD. Every day, decision makers operate their businesses with allocation-based cost systems. They make decisions that often are based on the assumption that the more that is done, the cheaper it is—make more, buy more, stock more because it is cheaper. This simply cannot be true. As more is done, costs are at least the same, if not more. In the case of the $8.00-per-hour worker, making the $n + 1$st unit cannot cost less. The worker is not being paid a lower hourly wage; rather, more materials and energy are consumed to produce the $n + 1$st unit than the nth unit.

Exhibit 2.6   Comparing Unit Cost and Bottom-Line Cost Dynamics

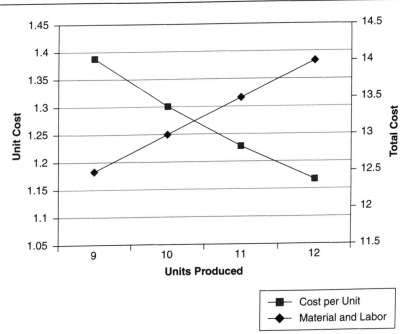

The confusion stems, fundamentally, from how costs are defined. If costs are purposely tied to a unit of production, allocation is required, which leads to conclusions such as the more someone makes, the less costly it is. Two different issues are being addressed here. The problem is that total cost and unit cost both are costs and are, therefore, confused. A unit cost, if it exists, is not synonymous with total costs, however. By assuming that they are the same, managers risk increasing their costs by trying to become more efficient. To eliminate this confusion, ECD eliminates the concept of a unit cost so that there is no ambiguity when discussing costs and cost dynamics.

Herein lies the difference between ECD and traditional allocation systems. ECD does not recognize allocations in any way. The framework focuses on recognizing how costs behave vis-à-vis the bottom line. The measures discussed throughout the book are developed directly from the bottom line. Therefore, when a decision is made, the bottom-line impact is immediately known.[2]

Before closing this section, an essential point should be addressed regarding efficiency. Efficiency can be a good thing but not in the way traditionally considered. First, considering the previous production example where the worker had a standard of 10 units per hour, if there were market demand for 12 units per hour, increased efficiency brings more revenues, leading to increased profits. Profits, however, stem from more sales—not from lower costs. Second, lack of efficiency in and of itself is not more costly; instead, it depends on the situation. Assume a demand rate of nine units per hour. Being less efficient can actually increase profits (material costs are lower). If, however, the demand rate is higher than the production rate, managers may be forced to make a decision that might increase costs, such as the need to work overtime. Inefficiency may have led to this decision. It is the action resulting from this decision that determines whether costs increase or not. Increasing efficiency leads to a reduced need for these actions.

EXPLICIT COSTS AND IMPLICIT COSTS

Explicit Costs

Each company has an organization, and the financial activity of this organization is used to define the income statement. In ECD, the definition of the organization is the lowest level definable where an external income statement is created. Assume that someone were to draw an imaginary border around the organization (Exhibit 2.7). Every time money passes through the border and into the box, it is revenue to the organization, regardless of its source. Every time money passes away from the organization, it is a cost. When money passes through the border, it becomes an explicit flow. This is a basic assumption for ECD. The box discussed in this example is the Cost-Revenue Border (C-R Border, or CRB).

The C-R Border cannot be defined at a lower level than the organization for ECD to work. If the C-R Border were used to define a profit center, it is possible that costs could flow into and out of this profit center without being identifiable in the bottom line. Implicit costs and transfer costs are examples of cost flows that can occur at the profit center level and not be seen at the organization level. At this point, explicit flows are no longer being considered. Departments acting as profit centers could pass money back and forth without any dollars leaving the organization. If the C-R Border were used at too low a level, ECD could not ensure that bottom-line impacts would occur.

Exhibit 2.7 Only Money Coming Into and Leaving the C-R Border
Are Explicit

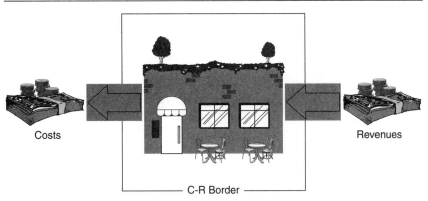

From this definition, profit is the difference between revenues
going into the organization and costs exiting the organization. To
determine the profit for an arbitrary period, the period is identified
and the revenues into the organization and the costs from the organization are determined. An arbitrary period can be defined. The
most important issue is to focus on explicit money flow during this
period. If the revenues exceed costs for the organization over the period, the impact is positive profit and, therefore, more money for the
company. Likewise, if the costs exceed the revenues, the available
money is reduced.

There is a relationship, therefore, between the revenues, costs,
and the money or cash flow that a company has. To lay the ground-
work for this relationship, consider the following example. Assume
that a person has $100.00 cash. The individual goes to work, is paid
$50.00, and subsequently pays $30.00 for bills. What is the person's
cash flow? It is now $120.00 (Exhibit 2.8). Each dollar is identifiable.

Exhibit 2.8 Cash That Does Not Exit the C-R Border Does Not
Have an Impact on the Cash Position of That Within
the Border

Situation	Initial Cash	Income	Expenses	Resulting Cash
Single	$100	$ 50	$30	$120
Married	$150	$120	$60	$210
Transfer	$150	$120	$60	$210

Exhibit 2.9   Which Costs Count, and Which Do Not?

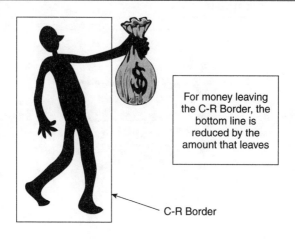

For money leaving the C-R Border, the bottom line is reduced by the amount that leaves

C-R Border

A direct relationship between profit and cash flow can exist. Now, assume that the person is married. The couple pools its resources, and together they have $150.00. One spouse is paid $50.00 and pays $30.00 in bills. His partner is paid $70.00 and pays $30.00 in bills. What is their total cash flow? His contribution to cash flow is $20.00, and his partner's contribution is $40.00. Therefore, the total contribution to cash flow is $60.00. They now have $210.00. Now assume that he owes his partner $20.00 for money borrowed previously. He gives the partner $20.00. What is the impact on the cash flow for the couple? Nothing. Because the transaction occurs within the family, it will not show up when considering the couple's financial holdings (Exhibit 2.9).

What happened from a mathematical perspective? The profit of the individual was the difference between their respective salaries and the bills that they had to pay.

$$\text{Profit} = \text{Salary} - \text{Bills}$$

The cash flow at the end of the transactions was equal to the cash flow before the transactions with the profit added to it.

$$\text{Cash Flow}_{\text{resulting}} = \text{Cash Flow}_{\text{initially}} + \text{Profit}_{\text{now}}$$

Where does the transaction representing the borrowed money come in? It does not if the analysis represents the couple. In this case, it is almost as if the husband took money out of his budget, assuming

Exhibit 2.10   Only If Dollars Leave or Enter the C-R Border Do
They Impact the Bottom Line

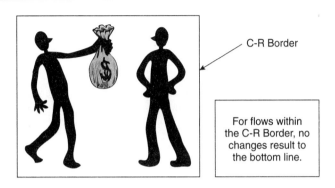

C-R Border

For flows within
the C-R Border, no
changes result to
the bottom line.

he had one, to pay his partner. Only money that comes into or goes
out of the C-R Border drawn around the couple has an effect on their
profit and, therefore, their cash flow (Exhibit 2.10).

When taken to the organization level, the same things occur.
First, the profit is equal to the difference between the revenues over
a period and the costs during the same period. The exact same equation applies. Second, the cash flow of the company is equal to the
cash flow at the beginning of the period added to the profit, whether
positive or negative, incurred over the analysis period. Budget transfers within the organization do not have an impact on the organization's cash flow.

Opportunity Costs

Implicit costs can be defined as the costs of nonpurchased inputs,
such as services received by one department within a company from
another department within the same company, for which a cash
value must be imputed because the inputs are not purchased in a
market transaction.[3] An opportunity cost is the cost of choosing to
use resources for one purpose measured by the sacrifice of the
next-best alternative for using those resources.[4] Both implicit costs
and opportunity costs are used by managers even though they are
not explicit. Opportunity costs are often assessed a cash value in order to feel comfortable that a thorough economic analysis has been
performed. The concern here is with how companies consider and,
therefore, use opportunity costs for decision-making purposes. Although a company may incur inputs that do not actually cause cash

Exhibit 2.11   Since Transfer Pricing Involves Transactions within the C-R Border, There Is No Direct BLI

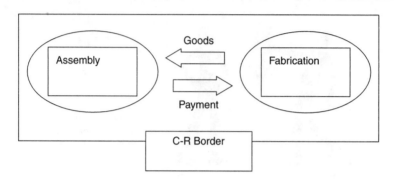

to flow, for decision-making purposes, these dollar values are some-times considered part of the total cost of a product, thus inflating the so-called unit cost. Transfer pricing is evidence of this behavior (Ex-hibit 2.11).

Opportunities cost nothing. What is lost in opportunity cost sit-uations is revenue. For instance, if a $100.00 investment at 8 percent interest compounded annually, in one year, the investment would be worth $108.00 (Exhibit 2.12). In a risk-free opportunity to invest the same $100.00 at 10 percent interest compounded annually over the same year, the investor could receive $110.00. Given the fact that the investor had the opportunity to make $10.00 versus $8.00, the situation is assumed to cost the investor a net of $2.00. Realisti-cally, it cost the investor, who actually made $8.00, nothing. Nonethe-less, the investment remains $100.00.

These opportunity costs exist in many measures used to make decisions, however. Production quantity equations, for example, consider the cost of back orders or stockouts. Loss of goodwill is sometimes cited as a cost of not having a product when someone wants to buy it. Since loss of goodwill has no direct effect on the dol-lars flowing out of the control volume (it could have a definite im-pact on future dollars flowing into the control volume), it will not change the costs that a company incurs.

If a client is disappointed that her favorite bookstore does not have a book she was told was in stock, for example, what is lost is the revenue for that particular book and potentially for more books, as she might take her business elsewhere. The argument could be made that whether the amount lost shows up as an increased cost or de-

Exhibit 2.12   Opportunity Costs Do Not Cost Anything

Opportunity	Investment	Growth Potential	Amount Forgone
Chosen	$100	$8	0
Passed	$100	$10	$2

creased revenue, the profit remains the same. This is true; the opportunity cost of not having a book in stock can be valued as the profit that would have resulted if it had been in stock and sold. However, not distinguishing between whether the lost profit came from missed revenue opportunities or from opportunity costs can lead to improper decisions regarding handling the particular issue to maximize profit. Mathematically, it does not really matter where the resources are put. However, from a management perspective, it does matter. It is similar to when a person looks upon something as a liability, not as an asset, it tends to change the way that person manages it. The individual manages *around* it, not *through* it.[5] Considering opportunity costs on the cost side of the equation can be very dangerous, for it creates a situation where it becomes difficult to distinguish between revenues and costs. Costs are managed differently than revenues. Emphasizing costs might lead to *don't-do management*—don't do any purchasing of new machines; don't do any hiring of new people; don't do anything that lets the machine sit idle. Emphasizing revenue and profit while managing costs, however, might lead to *do management*—perhaps we need to buy more machines to meet demand; perhaps we need more people because we cannot meet demand. These are two very different ways of handling what turns out to be the same problem.

EXPLICIT COST DYNAMICS COST DEFINITIONS

There are three cost types defined and used by ECD. Resource costs, action costs, and item costs are the building blocks on which ECD is built. Changes in each of these cost types are identifiable on the bottom line of the organization. Because of their direct ties to the bottom line, all measures used in the ECD framework will use these cost types or some subset of the cost types. As a result, managers will have a more concrete and forward-looking measurement system than is available with allocation-based costing systems (Exhibit 2.13).

Exhibit 2.13   The Usual Suspects

	Resource Costs	Action Costs	Item Costs
Unit rate(s)	\$ ÷ Time	\$ ÷ Time \$ ÷ Action	\$ ÷ Unit
Examples	Salaries Rent Insurance	Consulting fees Shipping	Direct and nondirect materials

Resource Costs

A resource cost is a cost that would exist if all activity stopped but the organization was still operable. In a case such as this, the company would have to continue paying salaries for the time worked, rent, general electricity, information-technology systems, and other infrastructural requirements of the organization. These are resource costs. Resource costs exist because they provide the fundamental capacity to do work. If nothing were sold, the company would still have people working, the building in which they work, and fundamental utilities.

Resource costs will usually have time-based unit rates. Salaries, unless paid by piecework, are resource costs. Employees are usually paid based on salaries that are hourly based, monthly based, or yearly based. If the employees were standing around doing nothing, the company would still incur these costs. The same goes for any other cost that is independent of the activities within an organization.

Action Costs

Action costs are costs incurred by performing a particular action. Action costs usually have either a time-based unit rate or an action-based unit rate. Examples of action costs are freight costs, long-distance costs, and setup costs. When the action is performed, the bottom-line cost increases by the product of the unit rate and the frequency of occurrence of the action.

Item Costs

When an organization buys something that subsequently can be sold, it has purchased an item. Item costs clearly will have item-based unit rates. The more items purchased, the higher the item cost.

WHY IS ECD NECESSARY?

As was discussed in Chapter 1, current accounting systems create confusion and ambiguity in their use. There is no assurance that either a negative or positive BLI will occur when using measures based on arbitrary allocations. This confusion—ambiguity tied to the arbitrary—increases the probability that a decision will cause either a less than desirable BLI or, in some cases, a completely undesirable BLI. Decision making should be based on tools that can be counted on to provide the results that they suggest. Every day, disagreements occur in organizations because of issues that result from allocation-based cost accounting systems. ECD aims to eliminate this frustration and to provide everyone in an organization with the relevant information to make a decision and to understand the BLI of the decisions made.

Endnotes

[1] David N. Hyman, *Economics,* 3rd ed. (Burr Ridge, IL: Irwin, 1994), p. 208.

[2] Independently of other activities, ECD does not take the place of a manager who has to understand interactions of projects, programs, or activities.

[3] Hyman, *Economics,* p. 197.

[4] Hyman, *Economics,* p. 9.

[5] Robert H. Hayes, Steven C. Wheelwright, and Kim. B. Clark, *Dynamic Manufacturing: Creating the Learning Organization* (New York: The Free Press, 1988), p. 16.

3

Understanding Explicit Cost Dynamics Costs

Explicit cost dynamics (ECD) creates a somewhat different paradigm for understanding costs. It redefines costs to establish integrity between the decisions made with ECD tools, techniques, and the bottom line. This chapter introduces the concepts necessary to create the ECD framework and to begin to understand ECD in more detail.

Cost levels focus on the relationships between costs and how the organization incurs the costs. Cost types are those costs that the organization incurs within a cost level. Together, cost levels and cost types form the basis for a cost management system that does not need allocation. Additionally, in this chapter, cost focus shifts to the total cost function. The total cost function represents the sum of all costs incurred and represents the total cost value used to determine profitability. This chapter shows how each cost type and each level directly feeds the value for total cost. The discussion then shifts to the total cost function as a function that exists in a multidimensional cost space. Because multiple independent costs make up the total cost function, it is impossible to represent total cost as a function in three cost dimensions or less. Finally, the chapter closes with discussion regarding techniques for managing total cost in the ECD space.

COST DYNAMICS

Chapter 2 introduced three types of costs at a high level: (1) resource costs, (2) action costs, and (3) item costs. This section introduces the concept of a cost level, describes the types of costs in more detail, and identifies characteristics of costs that allow them to fall into the defined categories.

Cost Levels

There is a point below which an organization cannot further break down costs without arbitrary assumptions and approximations. This is the *cost level*. There are three cost levels (1) program level, (2) superprogram level, and (3) resource level (Exhibit 3.1). Cost levels allow managers to understand why and where the organization incurs costs.

A relationship exists between a cost type and a cost level in that a cost level represents activities within an organization. If an organization takes on a new product or service or chooses to perform an internal activity, this activity will dictate the level of the costs that the program incurs. As the organization incurs costs, the cost types represent the usage and dynamics of the cost. The organization cannot break down costs incurred for a specific situation below their intended cost level. To do so is to allocate, which is against the fundamental premises of ECD.

A one-to-many relationship exists between the use of cost types at a given cost level. In other words, multiple cost types might make up one cost level. A relationship also exists for the mapping of cost types to cost levels; again, multiple cost levels may exist for one cost type (Exhibit 3.2). Although to determine which level a cost belongs depends on the application of the cost type, an individual cost type will not cross levels within one application.

Program Level

A program consists of a set of activities, actions, and items that meet certain organizational goals or objectives. A program might consist of designing a product, fulfilling an order, or performing services for a client. Assume, for instance, that an organization must purchase 10

Exhibit 3.1   Three Major Cost Levels

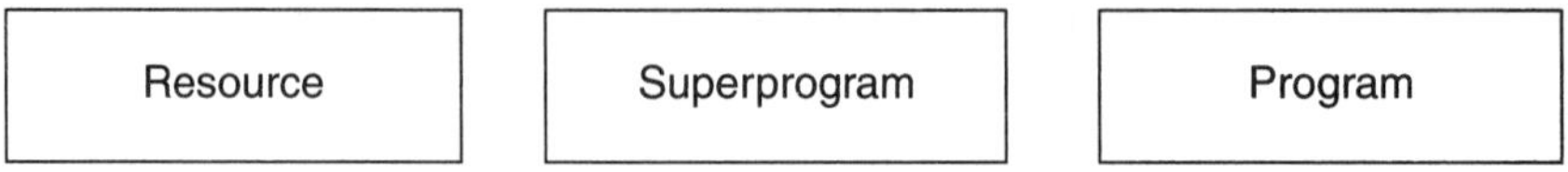

Resource	Superprogram	Program

Exhibit 3.2   Each Cost Type Can Be Associated with One or More
                Cost Levels

Cost Type	Cost Levels Available
Item	Program Superprogram Resource
Action	Program Superprogram Resource
Resource	Resource

motors to fulfill an order for a batch of fans that the organization is about to manufacture. If the organization purchased these items to meet existing demand (the order exists but the inventory necessary to meet the order has not yet been procured), the associated action is tied to fulfilling an order. The order in this case is the program.

Superprogram Level

The superprogram level consists of multiple programs. For example, an organization might buy 10 motors at one time for two existing orders. Each order might be a program, and the motors are for the fans that will make up the two orders. The organization may incur costs, such as order costs and shipping costs, from ordering all parts at once. However, the cost of ordering all 10 motors at one time is not allocable. Why? Again, because the allocation technique is still arbitrary even though the allocation seems straightforward. What happens, for instance, if the organization places the order, receives the motors, and a client cancels one of the orders? Who incurs what costs? Should the remaining client cover the order cost? If an organization wanted to allocate the order cost, what basis should it use? Percent of total motors?

Resource Level

The resource level is the highest cost level that exists, for costs in this level are associated only with the organization. Regular employees are examples of resource-level costs. Although they might be working on a specific program, engineers are also organization employees;

if the organization eliminated the program they are working on, it would still have the resource cost. Temporary employees who may be working on the same program, however, may not be resource-level costs. If these employees work only on the program and if their jobs end upon completion of the program, they would be program or superprogram costs.

It is not enough to say that a particular cost is always at the same level, however. To illustrate this point and to show how the cost level can change, consider a single shipment that an organization chooses to deliver products to its customer using a trucking company.

Scenario 1. The truck used for shipping contains one item from one order. This may be the case when shipping a large item such as a steel coil. In this instance, the shipping cost is associated with the order. Since the order is likely to be associated with one program, the cost is a program-level cost. The cost level in this case is the program level since the item is moving from one location to another and any cost associated with this transportation exists because of the needs of the order. If, however, the organization ships two coils, the cost level may move up one level, as is evident in the next scenarios.

Scenario 2. A truck has a load consisting of one order and multiple items. Assume further that the trucking company charges one price to make the shipment. The cost level in this case is the program. To break down the shipping cost to the unit level requires allocation approximations that lead to nonexistent cost behavior. For example, if the shipment has 1,000 units and a shipping employee decides to take one unit from the truck, the other units now carry a higher cost because there are fewer units to which the organization can allocate the costs. Assuming all the inputs associated with manufacturing those products are the same, an item costs more because someone made a decision to remove an item. Additionally, costs have not changed because the cost to ship the order will remain the same. If the organization must still send the one unit taken from the truck, the freight costs do not make that one item more expensive; they make the order cost increase. Therefore, the objective would be to ensure that the revenues generated by the order exceed the cost to produce and deliver the order.

Scenario 3. The truck has three orders of the same product and charges a flat rate for the shipment. The cost level in this case would be the three orders, or the *superprogram*, since the cost to ship would be the same regardless of the number of orders. To determine a shipping cost for a particular order would require taking the shipping cost to a subcost level, which involves assumptions and approximations that are arbitrary and potentially leads to troublesome conclusions. If the organization attempted to divide the cost into the three orders, it again would create nonexistent cost behavior and a situation that ultimately suboptimizes decisions.

In each case, attempting to assess costs at a level lower than its natural cost level leads to an inappropriate representation of costs. Allocation ratios create an opportunity to either manipulate the numerator (dollars) or the denominator (units), leading to the belief that the organization is minimizing costs when, in fact, costs remain the same or increase.

COST TYPES

Chapter 2 introduced cost types. The following sections, which discuss cost types in more detail, provide a deeper context regarding what the costs are, how organizations incur the costs, and how to manage the costs.

Resource Costs

The definition of a resource cost is a cost that will exist whether or not the organization performs any activities, purchases items, or sells goods. Resource costs must be paid regardless of what activity the resource is performing. They include any payments that the organization must make for rented facilities, even if the facilities currently are not used by the organization. Resource costs can also consist of infrastructure costs and annuity payments that, again, are independent of whether activities occur or not.

Resource costs are often constant throughout a graphical region, which, in this case, represents a range of values for the independent variable. Therefore, time might consist of a graphical region, and space might be another. When an organization exceeds the region for which the cost is at a constant value, the costs will often change in steps. For example, assume that an organization pays $10,000.00 per month for a warehouse. As shown in Exhibit 3.3, if the space provided by the warehouse is exceeded by, for example, 50,000 square feet, the organization will need to find another warehouse. The same situation occurs when the inventory exceeds the constraint of 100,000 square feet (two *small* warehouse locations).

Exhibit 3.3   Warehouse Costs as Step Functions

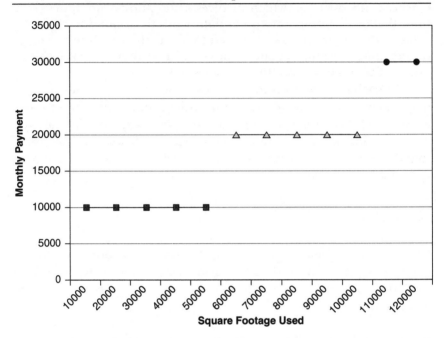

One very important issue to note is that regardless of what is in the warehouse, the cost is the same throughout the identified graphical region. Therefore, if one item is in the warehouse or several items are in the warehouse, until one exceeds the space requirements, total warehouse costs are equal. Again, this is not intuitive in a cost allocation paradigm, with which a typical approach might be to try to allocate the warehouse costs or the cost of storage to the cost of a unit of production. In addition to altering cost dynamics, managers must look into the past at activities that have occurred to be able to allocate the costs dynamically. In other words, managers must also wait until the activity is complete before being able to develop an arbitrarily allocated cost. Over time, managers can plan the utilization of these resources with the understanding that within a given region on the resource cost graph, costs will not vary. This allows managers to look forward when making decisions that involve these resources.

Resource costs can also appear to increase linearly. For example, a resource paid by the hour will realize a pay increase as the number of hours or fractions of an hour increase. The pay appears

Exhibit 3.4   Regardless of the Length of the Analysis Period, Costs
Still Occur as Discrete Units

Hourly rate	$8.00
Rate per minute	$0.13
Rate per second	$0.0022
Rate per millisecond	2.22×10^{-6}

to be linear in some cases because each period, in theory, is reducible
to the point where the cost function almost appears continuous (Exhibit 3.4). On further review, however, these costs are step functions
also. If an employee is paid by the hour and this is the lowest level at
which that person is paid (pay is not received for portions of an hour,
for example), the cost increases only if the organization hires another person or the original person works an additional hour.

In addition, ECD makes certain cost-oriented decisions easy.
For example, ECD points out that for most practical purposes, there
is a recommended method regarding how an organization might pay
a resource. It is cheaper to pay the resource by the hour than by the
half hour, and it is cheaper to pay the resource by the half hour than
by a tenth of an hour (Exhibit 3.5). With a more keen understanding of cost dynamics, these types of options and the optimal solutions
are clearer to the manager.

An organization's total resource costs are very important to determine, for an organization incurs these costs whether resources are
active or not. This is a large cost value that the profits from programs
incurs (discussed in the measures section) must recover to ensure
overall profitability. Organizations often apply these costs as overhead or as a burden charge to products and programs when using
typical accounting systems. In contrast, ECD defines resource costs
and uses them as part of a benchmark for programs to recover. Instead of allocating these costs, they remain as costs associated with
doing business. Organizations must recover these costs by effectively
pricing products and services and not by increasing the perceived
cost through arbitrary allocations. The pricing of products becomes
one of recovering the cost of developing and delivering the product
(program-level costs as well as a portion of the costs of doing business) rather than allocating the cost of doing business.

To determine total resource cost, simply add the organization's
expected resource costs for a period. This calculation can look

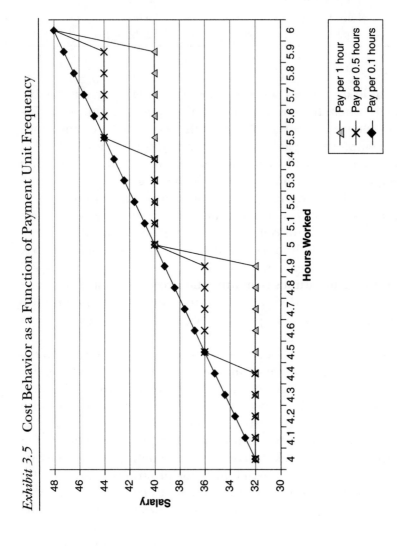

Exhibit 3.5 Cost Behavior as a Function of Payment Unit Frequency

backward to determine variances. It can also look forward as managers attempt to determine what resource costs will exist over a period in order to increase profitability through effective management and pricing.

Mathematically, Equation 3.1 expresses the total resource cost.

$$Rc_i = \Sigma \text{ (Individual Resource Costs over Period } i) \qquad (3.1)$$

Rc is the total resource cost over period i. The individual resource costs represent the resource costs that the organization will incur over period i. Upon identifying the period i, the larger i is, the more likely the resource costs are to be constant. Can they vary? Of course. However, over a three-month period, salaries are assumed to be constant. Based on expected demand placed on the organization, managers can determine what capacity will be necessary. This information allows organizations to plan using constant costs. The information is also available for future-planning purposes, thus creating the basis for a forward-looking cost management system.

Action Costs

Many of an organization's costs are action costs, or costs incurred on a regular basis as resources perform their work. For example, as a worker sets out to do a job, any costs associated with performing those duties are likely to be action costs. Action costs are associated with a program when the organization incurs these costs only with respect to that specific program. When shipping a product by truck, for example, ECD ties the cost of shipping to the cost of filling the order that the items are to meet. However, if an LTL (less than truckload—a shipping situation where a shipment does not fill an entire truck) creates an opportunity to ship another order, the cost for the truck is not allocable. Why? How would an organization allocate the costs? It could allocate based on area, volume, weight, number of units, and so on. Whichever method the organization chooses, however an argument can be made against it. If, by chance, one allocation base becomes the standard, there is still the problem of whether allocation really represents true cost dynamics. In the ECD framework, allocation misrepresents true cost dynamics.

There are ways of dealing with the problem without allocating the cost. What are the gains of shipping two orders on one truck? The organization will not incur costs associated with two shipments. If the organization priced both orders to include shipping, combining orders reduces the planned shipping action cost. This benefit goes straight to the bottom line as a cost avoidance through efficient management. The organization may still price each order as if the shipment must take place individually and achieve profit by only shipping once. Another option would be to keep the cost at the level of both orders without allocating (the superprogram level).

Item Costs

Item costs are functions of the number of items purchased; they are not a direct function of how the item is used. It is very important to draw a distinction here. If items are to be used in production, the actual procurement of the items is often independent of the number of units produced. The proof that they are independent is the fact that many companies have low raw material inventory turns or problems with obsolescence, both of which suggests too much inventory. If there were a direct relationship, obsolescence would not exist, since all items purchased are to be used. Likewise, inventory turns would be very high because only enough inventory exists to meet the demand.

Ideally, managers should procure at a rate directly tied to the demand. They would, in essence, attempt to force dependency between item cost and units produced. The need for this forced dependency led to the development of pull-type inventory management systems. By pulling inventory, the organization only buys what it consumes. With push-type inventory systems, the organization bases the procurement rate on a forecast that is, fundamentally, a guess.

With allocation cost systems, however, creating the direct dependency between demand and order quantities becomes difficult. Take, for example, the whole concept of economic order quantities; these algorithms focus on obtaining the lowest item cost. An organization may determine an optimal order quantity based on the need to balance inventory costs, which increase with the amount of inventory, and order costs, which, believers suggest, decrease as an organization purchases more items. Since it should be understood that costs cannot go down as an organization does more, these developments should automatically create skepticism. Continuing, however, the math of economic order quantities tries to find the right balance to minimize unit cost. Once determined, companies often push buyers to order in these economic quantities. If there is not a direct tie between demand and consumption, how can the organization ensure that inventory, and therefore costs are at a desirable level?

Manufacturing management also use economic order quantities to determine optimum batch sizes. This use balances inventory costs (increasing with increasing units) with setup costs (decreasing cost with increasing units). The belief, again, is that the more items made with one setup, the lower the setup cost allocated to each item. Understanding of this concept is so pervasive that to even suggest that this may not be true can dismiss the adversary's credibility on the shop floor by those who spend every day in that environment. In fact, workers often take it upon themselves to combine batches with similar setups to save setup cost without regard to any downstream disruptions in product flow. Consider, for example, the plant operator mentioned in Chapter 1, who combined batches at his station to reduce the setup cost for the first operation. Recall this created a chaotic situation for heat treat. As the parts arrived in the wrong sequence the ovens remained idle as the temperatures changed to accommodate the parts that were waiting for processing. It is easy to question how much money the organization saved by this operator's action.

While the thought process of the operator is common, it is not necessarily good for business. Clearly an organization does not want to spend more money than it has to. However, if decisions lead to high levels of inventory, high inventory costs, and poor management of working capital, the organization might want to reconsider whether these "cost optimization" concepts work. In fact, one of the fathers of JIT, Shigeo Shingo, believed that the economic order quantity concept does not work. He offered that the economic order quantity measure is "an evasive measure and in no way a positive approach to production."[1] Given their management approaches, many leading manufacturers agree.[2]

How does ECD handle item costs? It depends on why and when the organization buys the items. Some markets require quick response, where having inventory ahead of demand allows the organizations to compete in their respective space or, in some cases, to have an advantage. In the case where an organization orders items in anticipation of demand, management makes the decision to stock inventory. The item costs are independent of the demand; the demand might materialize, it might not materialize, or it will be somewhere in the middle. What the demand will actually be is an unknown. Therefore, the organization chooses to make a decision to buy items, hoping that the demand will materialize. What if it does not? Should the price of other items assume the burden of managing the unknown or, in some cases, the burden of poor management? Items purchased to help meet future demand become resources. Even if the organization does nothing, it will retain the cost of the items as resources. To determine the resource cost, calculate the item cost and the cost associated with owning the inventory (Equation 3.2).

Item Resource Cost = f(Order Cost, Inventory Carrying Cost)   *(3.2)*

The same rule applies for items often called nondirect items or items that companies use that do not go into the production of a product. Examples range from computers to uniforms to pencils. These items are resource costs and are managed as such. Each computer, each uniform, and each pencil exists whether the employees perform work or not. Clearly, the more work that is done, the more pencils are needed. However, the decision to buy more pencils is a management decision related to how the appropriate manager handles the respective resource costs.

Another example of how ECD handles costs is an organization that purchases materials to meet existing demand. For example, certain types of construction outfits purchase materials just in time for use. These organizations incur the material costs to meet the demand placed on them. They do not hold inventory; rather, they buy it and use it right away. In this case, the total item cost becomes more like an activity at the program level. When building a house, the contractor buys the garage door of choice. When pricing the house, the activity associated with buying a garage door becomes easily identifiable as a cost associated with building one particular house; there is no ambiguity.

In the ECD framework, it is the cost level that will create the context for profit and cost management, which are also the bases for the measures used in the ECD framework. Managing intraprogram cost dynamics will help companies understand what costs the program incurs so that the program can be effectively priced and profitability ensured.

TOTAL COST

To ECD, total costs and the total cost function are very important, for the total cost determined by the total cost function is subtracted from revenues to determine bottom-line profitability. By using total cost to develop its ideas and measures, ECD ensures integrity with the bottom line as the framework is used to manage organizations. There are two ways to determine total cost: one way is to sum cost levels, and another is to sum cost types. Both ways produce the same answer, but one picks a technique to gain specific information. For example, a company may want to understand total cost by cost type. Information desired might include the contribution of actions to the total cost. In this case, the company would sum by cost type. If a company wants to know the impact of programs on total cost, it can sum by level. For the rest of this chapter, summation by type is the standard.

To determine the bottom-line cost over any given period, all costs paid in the analysis period are summed (see Equation 3.3). The costs paid in an analysis period might be different from the costs incurred by the payment method. An organization can buy a $100,000.00 computer in one month yet pay for it over twelve months. From a cost management perspective, the equal payments are the cash flowing away from the organization. Financial accounting may handle this separately. This is fine, for financial accounting and cost management have two separate roles with different assumptions and different usage.

$$\text{Total Cost}_{\text{Period}} = \Sigma(\text{Resource Costs})_{\text{Period}} + \Sigma(\text{Action Costs})_{\text{Period}} + \Sigma(\text{Item Costs})_{\text{Period}} \qquad (3.3)$$

TOTAL COST AS A MULTIDIMENSIONAL FUNCTION

Users often represent costs graphically. When considering a significant amount of data or when trying to identify trends in data, a two-dimensional graph to represent the data is often plotted. This type of representation is very common. Cost benefit analyses, for instance, plot increasing costs and increasing revenues and provide instant feedback on issues such as when the organization is operating in the red, when it is operating in the black, and when costs and revenues will be equal—the so-called break-even point. Graphical representation is ideal for this type of analysis. The difficulty, however, occurs when two and even three dimensions are no longer sufficient to represent these curves.

Costs in their purest form are two-dimensional functions. As discussed in Chapter 2, the cost function creates a line in two-dimensional space (or two-space). To recap, each cost function will have a unit rate. The unit rate serves as the slope of the cost curve. The amount of increase is based on how often, how long, or how many of the base unit are involved. When managers make decisions, however, they combine many of these cost functions, each of which is in two-space, to determine total costs. These managers may need to understand what combination of two or more variables provides the best solution at the right cost and profit level. Therefore, the representation must provide visibility into all total cost options so that an effective decision is made. The total cost function remains a true function—input the independent variables (time, actions, items) into the total cost function, and the function determines the one total cost. The problem is this: as multiple cost functions are combined in two-space, a two- and often three-dimensional graphic representation is no longer sufficient for representing the total cost of the function. Total cost functions become more and more complex, leading to the necessity to represent costs in four-space, five-space, and up to n-space.

Consider the following example of how this process might work and how rapidly three-space is eclipsed by simple scenarios. An organization creates a program to purchase up to five items at a cost of $500.00 each. Equation 3.4 is used to represent the cost of purchasing items, and Exhibit 3.6 is a graphical representation of this linear function.

$$\text{Total Item Cost} = \$500.00/\text{Item} \times \text{Number of Items} \qquad (3.4)$$

To determine the specifications, a team must visit the vendor to discuss issues with the vendor sales representatives and engineers. Each visit to the vendor costs $250.00. The function representing travel costs is displayed in Equation 3.5.

$$\text{Total Item Cost} = \$250.00/\text{Visit} \times \text{Number of Visits} \qquad (3.5)$$

Exhibit 3.7 shows the representation of the travel costs in two-space. Clearly, in both cases, the two-space representation adequately represents the cost curve. The difficulty arises when an attempt is made to determine the total cost for the program. Assume that management wants to determine the bottom-line cost for purchasing these items. The total cost would involve combining two independent variables into one cost function. The representation of this cost function becomes somewhat complicated. Two visits, for instance, can be coupled with the purchase of one, two, three, four, or five items. The total cost is now a function of the contribution of each cost function. In this case, the cost function requires a graphical representation in three-space. Exhibit 3.8 is a surface in three-space

Exhibit 3.6   Total Item Cost Increases as More Items are Purchased

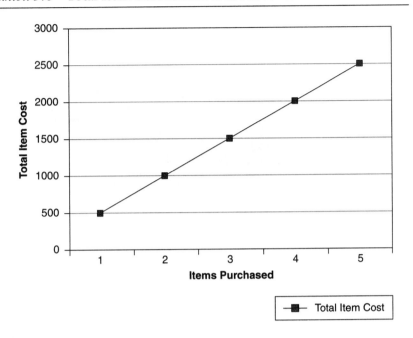

Exhibit 3.7   Total Travel Cost Increases with Increased Number of Trips

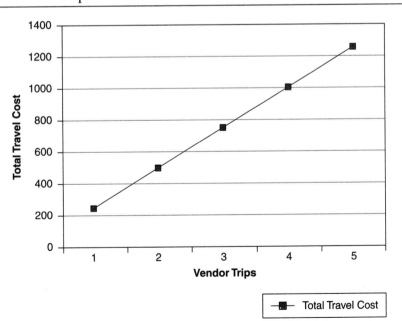

Exhibit 3.8   Total Cost of Purchase Activity

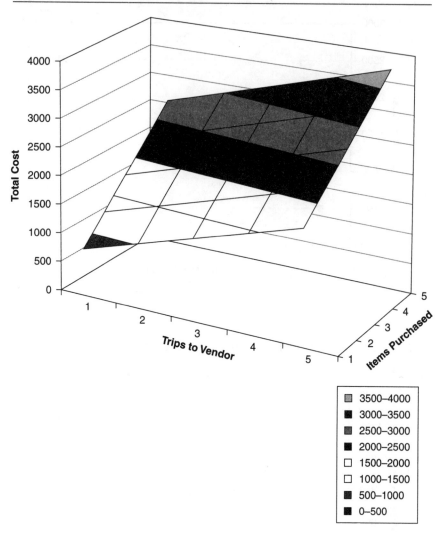

▨	3500–4000
◼	3000–3500
◼	2500–3000
◼	2000–2500
☐	1500–2000
☐	1000–1500
◼	500–1000
◼	0–500

that represents the combination of the visit function and the item function. The total cost surface, in this case, represents the total cost space possible for the program. Once the combination of independent variables is established (three visits and two items purchased), the total cost function determines the total cost ($2,250.00).

Although there is more to discuss in regard to this example, the essential point has been made. Costs are often independent and, when brought together, create the need to represent the data in n-space, where n is usually greater than two.

Managing Cost Functions

Many costs are independent of each other and are tied together only through a choice to bring them together. Consider the cost to produce an item and the cost to ship that item. The cost to produce the item will exist regardless of whether or not the item is shipped. True, the shipping cost would not exist if there were no item to ship; there is a relationship there. However, the company can choose to have the client pick the item up (no shipping), to send it via ground mail (some cost), or to send it via express mail (some cost greater than ground mail). The costs incurred to deliver the product are independent of the cost of producing the item. This becomes more evident when the production of a batch of these items is considered. Assume that 100 of the items were produced. The shipping costs and, therefore, the total cost are determined by the method chosen to ship the products. All could be sent via express mail, by some combination of all forms, or even not at all.

There is a variable component associated with the production of an item. As more of that item is produced, the cost associated with production increases. Therefore, an equation and, thus, a graph that represents the cost of producing the item can be created (Equation 3.6).

$$PC = f(\text{Units}) \qquad (3.6)$$

where PC = production cost.

This equation will be monotonically increasing, meaning that under no circumstances can a company produce more items and have the cost go down. It physically makes no sense to assume that it is less costly to produce 1,000 units than it is to produce 10.

Assuming that this relationship is linear, the production cost is represented as a line in a two-dimensional graph. With the units being the independent variable, the dependent variable, production cost, increases as the number of units produced increases (Equation 3.7).

$$PC = \frac{\text{Cost}}{\text{Unit}} \times \text{Units Produced} \qquad (3.7)$$

For shipping, a very similar situation exists. The transportation costs (TC) might be a function of the number of times an organization chooses to ship (Equation 3.8). Shipping can also be a function of weight, distance, and/or urgency, but for this case, it is frequency. The cost to ship the $n + 1$st time must be at least the cost of the nth time, suggesting that transportation, too, monotonically increases.

$$TC = g(\text{Shipments}) \qquad (3.8)$$

To determine the program cost in this scenario, both the production costs and the shipping costs must be known. Equation 3.9 shows how to represent the variable costs in this situation.

$$COST_{Total} = PC + TC$$

or

$$C(\text{Units, Shipments}) = PC + TC$$
$$= f(\text{units}) + g(\text{shipments}) \qquad (3.9)$$

The fact that the variables are independent leads to the following postulates:

- **Postulate 1** Because there exists the potential for multiple independent costs, there is no meaningful way to allocate a portion of each of these costs to the cost of a unit to create a unit cost.

- **Postulate 2** The independent variables creating the basis for the total cost function are different, suggesting that a graphical representation in a space larger than two dimensions is necessary to observe true cost dynamics. The representation of costs usually cannot be a line but a surface in a multidimensional space.

- **Postulate 3** Given the fact that the cost equations increase monotonically, the true low-cost solution is arrived at through reducing the value of the independent variables with *all* equations.

Postulate 1: Allocating Independent Costs Leads to Meaningless Information

In the case examined previously, total cost is the dependent variable, suggesting that both the number of units and the number of shipments must be known to determine its value. However, the cost to produce a unit or a batch of units is determined solely by the costs associated with producing the units and not by allocating other costs.

Consider the following situation. An organization builds units to stock in inventory for shipment when orders are received. The costs associated with producing the units are determined upon the completion of the program to build the units. Once the items are completed, the actual production cost has been determined. Regardless of how long the items have been on the shelves, the material and energy costs have already been determined. If an order comes in for a unit that requires shipping costs to be incurred, these costs *do not affect* the costs associated with producing any unit of the batch that was made. The shipping affects the total cost of filling the order. To allocate these independent costs unnecessarily distorts the production cost of the item, potentially to the point of leading to poor marketing and sales decisions. Allocation creates a value that does not mean anything. The cost to produce an item is the price to produce it and is independent of other variables such as shipping costs or other nonrelated costs.

Postulate 2: Total Costs Cannot Be Represented Fully in Two Dimensions

To determine program costs, both a production component and a shipping component are needed. To understand the dynamics of total costs in this example, its value should be represented as a combination of two functions: (1) production and (2) shipping. For a given number of units, multiple total cost values can exist due to the options available with shipping, suggesting that the mandatory one-to-one relationship for functions does not exist as if the dependent variable (total cost) is a function of units only. To completely represent this simple scenario and to fully understand the cost dynamics requires three dimensions. True, a value for shipping can be chosen—two, for example—and the three-dimensional space can be reduced to two dimensions, as the shipping cost will now be a constant. However, this approach becomes tedious when comparing multiple shipping cost alternatives and may not provide adequate information when the number of independent variables increases significantly.

Postulate 3: The True Low-Cost Solution Is Achieved Only through Reducing the Value of the Independent Variables That Make Up the Total Cost Function

Because costs monotonically increase, the lowest cost solution will occur when all of the independent variables are at a minimum. The issue then becomes not how to lower cost but how to manage costs for optimum profit.

MANAGING TOTAL COST

Managing costs as multidimensional functions is not the easiest task, but the techniques are straightforward. It is not possible to visualize a five-dimensional cost. The key is to not allocate costs; since the costs are often independent, the allocation leads to information that is less than optimal. Also, remember that cost functions are either constant, as in the case of the intraregional portion of a step resource function, or monotonically increasing. A cost per unit that includes any allocated cost (including direct labor), for instance, is meaningless and potentially harmful. Instead, the objective becomes to understand the independent costs that make up the total costs and to determine the total cost based on the total cost function. The objective in a situation other than in a pure production environment is not to reduce unit costs but to optimize the difference between the costs associated with a program and the revenues received from the program. Only by working with total costs (and not a form of allocated costs) can this determination be made.

OBJECTIVE OF COST MANAGEMENT

The objective of cost management is just that—cost management. One way to manage costs is to focus on incurring costs at a rate that sustains desired profitability. To accomplish this, organizations often refer to the idea of *cost minimization*. Because cost functions monotonically increase, cost minimization occurs when the organization is closed. Obviously, cost minimization should not be used, and the real objective is to find the right revenue and cost levels to maximize profits.

Another way to manage costs is to completely understand cost dynamics, including how the organization incurs costs and why the organization incurs costs. The cost level creates the proper context for this understanding. Once understood, it is up to managers to use their understanding of cost dynamics to make decisions and effectively manage their organization.

COSTS MUST STILL BE REDUCED

To manage costs, the issue of cost reduction will always exist. This is fine as long as the activity is a tool identified to increase profit (unless an organization is preparing itself to become a takeover target). Is cost reduction always a tool to increase profit? No. When the decision to reduce costs is independent of revenue maintenance or revenue increase, reducing costs independently may hinder the organization's ability to deliver the needed revenue to maintain or increase profitability. Organizations should start with the bottom line and try to figure out at an organization level what activities should occur to enhance profitability. Out of this global analysis, the organization should understand the impact that targeted cost reduction would have on the organization's ability to deliver.

Once an organization identifies and understands the targeted cost reduction, there are two ways to reduce costs. The first way is to incur fewer costs, which involves being at a lower value of the independent variable on the cost function graph. Exhibit 3.9 shows a lin-

Exhibit 3.9   Resource Costs Increase with Increased Resources

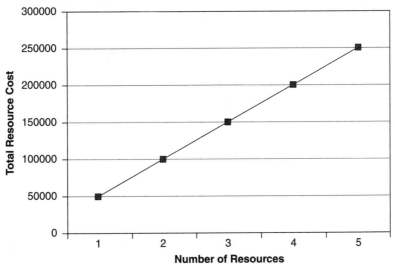

Exhibit 3.10   Action Costs Increase with Increased Occurrences

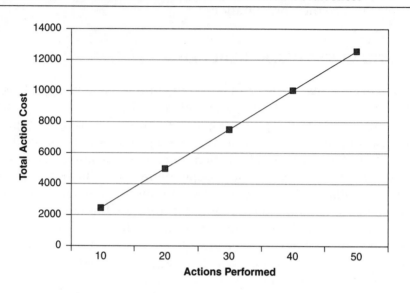

Exhibit 3.11   Total Cost Surface Represents Costs in Multiple
Dimensions

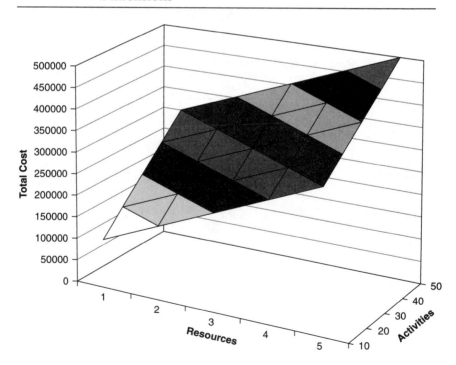

ear relationship between total resource cost and the number of resources. With fewer resources, the total cost is less.

Similarly, Exhibit 3.10 represents a relationship between actions
performed and total action cost. The fewer number of actions performed, the lower the cost. Notice that the low cost solution is to do
nothing and to have no resources.

The other way to reduce costs is to lower the unit rate of the
cost. Exhibit 3.11 is an example of an organization with $50,000.00
in resources performing actions. Notice on the curve that the fewer
resources and actions that the organization incurs, the lower the individual cost component. Exhibit 3.12 is the same as Exhibit 3.11 except that the resources are more expensive at $100,000.00 each. The
surfaces are parallel, with the surface in Exhibit 3.12 being shifted
upward by the increase in cost of the resources.

Shift, for a moment, into four-dimensional space. There are
three individual cost components making up total cost. The options

Exhibit 3.12   Total Cost Surface with Increased Resource Costs

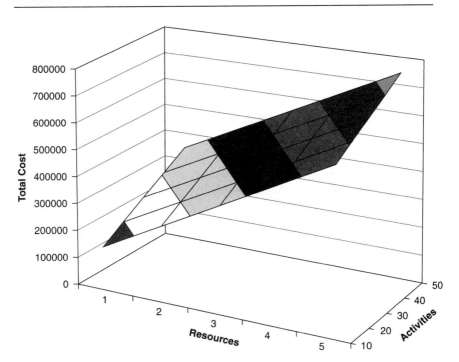

Exhibit 3.13   Options for Managing Total Cost Using the Total Cost
Surface

Lower Cost on a Curve	Lower Cost Surface
Do less	Lower the unit rate
Fewer items	Reduce the cost per item
Less time	Reduce the cost per activity
Fewer activities	Reduce the cost of each resource
Fewer resources	

to reduce costs are the same (Exhibit 3.13); they just cannot be seen. To reduce costs, an organization must either incur fewer costs or reduce the unit rate of the cost. When an organization gets into four-space and beyond, the surfaces no longer can be represented graphically. This does not mean that the same rules no longer apply. To aid in the analysis, however, the data from the organization's information system come in handy. With the data, an organization can perform what-if analyses on the cost-level functions to determine the impact of items, actions, and resources on the cost for that level.

Understanding the cost dynamics, however, is only a part of the equation. To manage profitability, organizations must take this cost information and consider revenue, and time to really get the full benefit of explicit Cost Dynamics.

Endnotes

[1]Shigeo Shingo, *A Revolution in Manufacturing: The SMED System,* trans. Andrew P. Dillon (1981; reprint, Boston: Productivity Press, 1985).

[2]Robert S. Kaplan, ed. *Measures of Manufacturing Excellence* (Cambridge: Harvard Business School Press, 1990).

4

Profit Dynamics

The concept of profit dynamics is an extension of the discussion in Chapter 2 about cost dynamics. When thinking about managing the organization, cost dynamics are not enough. Companies are not in business to minimize costs; they are in business to make money now and in the future.[1] Companies must manage costs within the context of optimizing profits. By introducing a revenue component to the dynamics of costs, the basis for profit dynamics is established.

Adding revenue dynamics to cost dynamics is not enough, however. There is a time component of profit dynamics that is critical in terms of understanding profit relationships between activities. As will be discussed throughout the next three chapters, events that happen within the context of profit dynamics are assumed to be related but in reality are not. One such example is product development. Organizations match the costs of development to the revenues received some time into the future to determine product-line or service-line profitability. Statements suggesting that products and services must be priced to recover past development costs are proof of this behavior. This, explicit cost dynamics argues, is not a reasonable practice given the profit dynamics of the situation. The reality is that although the costs and pricing are related, they are not totally dependent on each other.

There are three constitutive components of profit dynamics: (1) cost dynamics, (2) system dynamics, and (3) time. When the right aspects of each component are applied correctly, these components lead to a different and often insightful understanding of how activities and decisions affect the bottom line. This chapter will introduce system dynamics and time before developing the discussion of profit dynamics.

SYSTEM DYNAMICS AND TIME

Jay Forrester[2] introduced the concept of system dynamics as a scientific approach to understanding nonscientific systems and what influences them. He modeled these systems using basic components that seemed to represent the dynamics of a system. Forrester felt that many processes, activities, or phenomena could be modeled as closed systems. System dynamics could be used to model economic systems just as the duck population at a lake could be modeled. Two details are of most interest to this theory. First, a series of activities that in some way influence each other can be defined as a closed system. Second, there are components of system dynamics that apply to profit dynamics.

A closed system is often comprised of components, activities, and relationships that affect a variable of interest. For example, when modeling the duck population in a lake, components might be the condition of the lake, the temperature of the surroundings, the fish population, the insect population, the hostility of the environment toward ducks and ducklings, and so on. Ducks can come in from outside of the system just as they can leave the system. However, for modeling purposes, the lake can be effectively modeled as its own closed system.

Arguably, the most important component used to model closed systems is the level. Levels represent the state or condition of a closed system. The duck population might be a level when modeling a lake, just as the number of unemployed might be a level when modeling an economy.

A second important concept is the rate. Rates determine how a level changes with time (Exhibit 4.1). For example, birth rate and immigration rates of ducks will cause an increase in the population of ducks at the lake. The mortality rate and the emigration rate will decrease the population. Levels change based on the application of the

Exhibit 4.1   Levels and Rates Define the State of the System

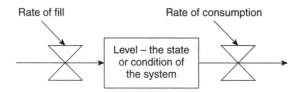

Exhibit 4.2   Only Ducks Entering and Exiting the System Affect the
Duck Population

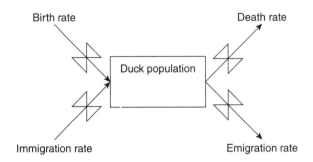

rate to the level. Thus, if the birth rate of ducks is 10 per month, the population increases by 10 per month. If the combination of mortality and emigration totals 7 ducks per month, the population decreases by 7 ducks. The net rate is the difference between the increase in ducks and the decrease in ducks, which is three in this case (Exhibit 4.2).

Rates do not have to be constant, however. Food, for example, may influence the duck population. If there is no food, the mortality rate and/or the emigration rate might increase sometimes to the point where the rate of decrease is greater than the rate of increase. If there is a significant amount of food at the lake, the environment may be able to support more ducks, which may increase the growth rates. Hostility might also influence the rate of decrease or increase. Many ducks might attract many hunters who kill the ducks at a rapid rate. Few ducks draw few hunters, which allows the population to increase. Many systems tend to oscillate; for example, abundant food might create a fast growth rate. As the population grows, the environment may not be able to provide enough food for the ducks, which can create a rapid decline in population until the environment becomes abundant with food again.

Overall, system dynamics is a very powerful tool with many uses and capabilities much beyond the scope of this book. Many of the fundamental principles described in Peter Senge's well-received book *The Fifth Discipline*[3] are based on system dynamics principles. It is important to utilize references such as this to learn more about how system dynamics can describe and help us manage the systems in which we operate every day.

To create a context for how system dynamics applies to profit dynamics, consider a very familiar model—a kitchen sink (Exhibit 4.3). The amount of water in the sink is the level in the closed system. Assume that someone is interested in measuring the amount of water in the kitchen sink at any given moment. The amount of water can be determined in many ways. One approach is to take measures to determine the amount of water in the sink. Another approach involves knowing the volume of water at some point in time, and by knowing the difference between the amount of water that has entered and the amount that has exited over a given period of time, the new water level can be determined. The latter approach is the approach more closely tied to system dynamics. It is more dynamic and provides insight into the water level in the past, in the present, and in the future. The system dynamics approach focuses on being able to answer the question of how much water is in the sink at any time and how it changes over time. This information describes the state of the system.

Over time, the amount of water in the sink will change by adding water or by taking it away. The amount added is determined by examining the rate at which the water comes in (for example, gallons per minute, or gpm) and the amount of elapsed time at this rate (minutes). Simply, if water flows in at a rate of 3 gallons per minute for two minutes, the level is now 6 gallons greater assuming no water has exited. The rate of exit affects the level similarly. For example, assume that there are 5 gallons of water in the sink. The faucet is turned on, and water begins to enter at a rate of 1.5 gpm. The water level will increase over time, as demonstrated in Exhibit 4.4. After five minutes, the amount of water is 12.5 gallons. At the rate of 1.5 gpm, 7.5 gallons entered the sink.

Assume now that the flow of water into the sink has stopped and that someone removes a stopper in the bottom of the sink. Wa-

Exhibit 4.3   A Sink as a Closed System

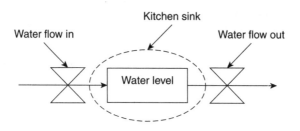

Exhibit 4.4   Representing the Level of Water Over Time

Time (minutes)	Cumulative Flow (gpm)	Total Water Level (gallons)
0	0	5
1	1.5	6.5
2	3	8
3	4.5	9.5
4	6	11
5	7.5	12.5

Exhibit 4.5   Effect of Rates and Time on Reducing the Water Level

Time (minutes)	Cumulative Flow (gpm)	Total Water Level (gallons)
0	0	5
1	−1	4
2	−2	3
3	−3	2
4	−4	1
5	−5	0

ter will exit the sink at an assumed rate of 1 gpm. As is apparent from Exhibit 4.5, the total amount of water will decrease at the same rate as water exits through the drain. By knowing the exit rate of the water, the water level can be determined at any time. Assuming that everything is equal, future levels also can be predicted. For example, it can be predicted that after two minutes, the water level will be 10.5 gallons.

What if water is coming into the sink and leaving the sink at the same time? What will happen to the water level? It depends. Exhibit 4.6 shows that the net rate at which water enters the sink determines what happens to the water level. If more water enters the sink than leaves, the water level will rise at the rate equal to the difference between the entry rate and the exit rate. This example can be experienced when taking a shower every morning. Hair clogging the drain reduces the exit rate of the water. If the rate of water entering the shower is faster, water begins to accumulate around the feet and hopefully not too much higher. If the rate out is greater, the water

Exhibit 4.6 Entry and Exit Rate Differences Determine Changes in Water Level

Time (minutes)	Entry Rate (gpm)	Exit Rate (gpm)	Net Flow Rate (gpm)	Cumulative flow (gpm)	Total Water Level (gal)
0	0	0	0	0	5
1	1.5	1	0.5	0.5	5.5
2	1.5	1	0.5	1	6
3	1.5	1	0.5	1.5	6.5
4	1.5	1	0.5	2	7
5	1.5	1	0.5	2.5	7.5

Exhibit 4.7 No Delta within a Period Leads to No Change in Water Level

Time (minutes)	Cumulative Flow (gpm)	Total Water Level (gallons)
0	0	5
1	0	5
2	0	5
3	0	5
4	0	5
5	0	5

level will decrease or remain negligible. If the rates are equal, the level of the water will remain the same (Exhibit 4.7).

Equation 4.1 summarizes these examples.

$$\text{Water Level}_{i+1} = \text{Water Level}_i + \text{Rate in}_{i+1} - \text{Rate out}_{i+1} \qquad (4.1)$$

What does this mean? The subscript i represents an arbitrary time period; it is a variable representing a moment in time, and i can be a day, week, month, year, or some other period. If i were equal to 2 in the above examples, it would refer to the 2-minute period. If i were 2, $i + 1$ would be 3. The water level is self-explanatory. In prose form, the equation states that the water level at some future time is equal to the sum of the water level during the preceding period and the net flow rate during the period in question (Equation 4.2). When the difference between the rate in and the rate out is determined, the result is the net flow rate (Equation 4.3).

$$\text{Water Level}_{i+1} = \text{Water Level}_i + \text{Net Flow Rate}_{i+1} \qquad (4.2)$$

$$\text{Net Flow Rate} = \text{Rate in} - \text{Rate out} \qquad (4.3)$$

Thus, for any period i, the future water level can be determined by adding the future net flow rate to the current water level. The essential point is the net flow rate for two reasons. The first reason is that the net flow rate, alone, changes the state of the system—the water level. The second reason is how the net flow rate constrains, along with time, managing the water level. To change the state of the system, the rates must be active or they must be changed. There are many approaches to change rates, but all approaches must go through the rate *mechanism* to influence the system.

The flow rates into and out of the sink do not have to be constant. The rate of entry into the sink can be slowed as the water level approaches the desired level. The dynamics of the system work the same. The rate for the given time period must be determined and decisions must be made based on this information. Consider the situation in which the net flow rate varies and the water level must be determined. Assume, for this example, that the net flow rate of 1 gpm increases at a rate of 0.5 gpm each minute (Exhibit 4.8). So, for the first minute, the rate is 1 gpm, the second is 1.5 gpm, the third 2 gpm, up to a maximum of 3 gpm at five minutes, as represented by the net flow rate and the net flow rate axis in Exhibit 4.9. To determine the change in the water level, the period must be identified and relevant rates of increase must be used to determine the actual water levels. For example, from Equation 4.2, the water level in time period 3 is equal to the sum of the water level in time period 2 (7.5 gallons) and the net flow rate in time period 3 (1.5 gpm). The level is 9 gallons. Only the net flow rate from time period 3 can

Exhibit 4.8   Net Positive Flow Rate Increases the Water Level

Time (minutes)	Net Flow Rate (gpm)	Total Water Volume (gallons)
0	0	5
1	1	6
2	1.5	7.5
3	2	9.5
4	2.5	12
5	3	15

Exhibit 4.9   Water Level with Variable Net Flow Rate

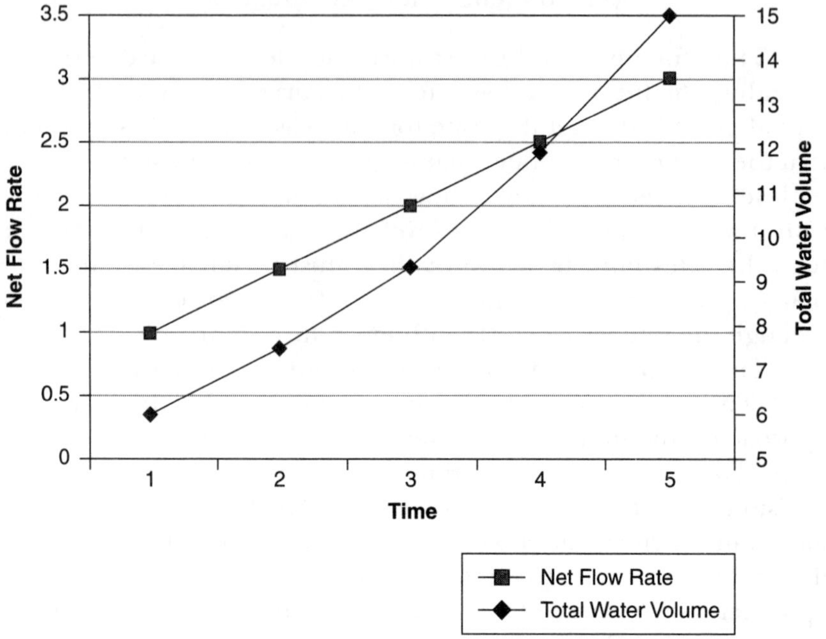

be used. It makes no sense to add to the water level in time period 2 the net flow rate from time period 4. (Remember how obvious this point is for discussion later in this chapter.)

So, what does this entire discussion on sinks and water have to do with profit? Replace the sink with the organization. This becomes the closed system for the analysis. Replace the water level with cash. This becomes the state of the system. Replace the rate of water in with revenues and the rate out with total costs. The result is the closed system, the level, and the rates in and out that change the level over time (Exhibit 4.10).

EXPLICIT PROFIT DYNAMICS

Explicit profit dynamics is the combination of revenues and total costs for the purpose of understanding the impact of each to the bottom line of the organization. Comparing to system dynamics, the organization's money is the level and the closed system is the organiza-

Exhibit 4.10   Representing Cash as the State of a System

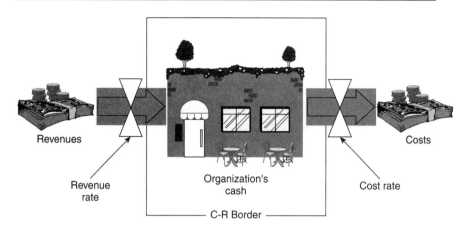

Revenues

Revenue
rate

Organization's
cash

Cost rate

Costs

C-R Border

tion. The system will measure everything entering and exiting the organization. Revenue is the rate of increase of cash, while costs reduce the amount of cash available. Together, they represent the fundamentals of profit dynamics.

Before combining all of the components to develop explicit profit dynamics, a couple of concepts must be discussed—the law of conservation of dollars and the issue of time. The law of conservation of dollars, a simple law that identifies what can and cannot be done while analyzing dollar flows, will be discussed first. Time, which is probably the most important issue in terms of managing an organization and its finances, will be examined next.

Law of Conservation of Dollars

The law of conservation of dollars suggests that an organization cannot create or destroy money. Governments can print money; organizations, however, cannot legally print money for their own use as legal tender. Therefore, all financial transactions must be identifiable and must balance. A cost reduction, for instance, should show up as a reduction of cash flowing away from the organization and should be identifiable when analyzing cash over time. This reduction occurs when analyzing the money dynamics of the organization. Costs cannot be reduced without the transaction being reflected as a reduction in the money flow away from the organization.

The law of conservation of dollars is important when using explicit profit dynamics because it creates the foundation for why explicit profit dynamics works. Unless cash enters or leaves the organization through the C-R Border, the bottom line and the cash remain the same. This concept will be very important when considering program management and cost justification activities. When money leaves the C-R Border, the effect is less cash. The transaction is easily identifiable, and the mathematics of the transaction supports the effects. Consider, however, a transfer of money from one budget to another. Since no money flows across the C-R Border and the cash for the organization does not change, this transaction does not affect the bottom line or the cash position of the organization. Everything remains the same at the organizational level. For the organization to be profitable, it must create money because no money crosses the border in this case. Although organizations continually transfer money between budgets and sell their own products to other departments within the organization assuming that the activities affect profits, the transactions have no direct effect on money and profits.

Common knowledge tells us that profit equals the difference between revenues and total costs (Equation 4.4). Therefore, the profit in a given period is equal to the difference between revenues and total costs in that period and in that period alone. The profit within that period determines how much of an increase or decrease the organization will see in its cash. If the profits for each period were added over a length of time including one or multiple periods, the money available to the organization at any given time could be determined. As defined by Equation 4.5, profit determines how much of a contribution to cash is made for a particular period. If an organization makes $10.00 profit for one period and $5.00 for the next, the contribution to the cash is $15.00 for the two periods.

$$\text{Profit} = \text{Revenue} - \text{Total Cost} \qquad (4.4)$$

$$\text{Avaliable Money}_j = \text{Available Money}_{\text{Time}=0} \sum_{\text{Time}=0}^{i} \text{Profit}_{\text{Time}} \qquad (4.5)$$

When performing analyses involving money, organizations must account for every dollar. If one dollar enters the organization, it enters as part of a revenue stream. The total costs during the period in which the money leaves the organization also must be identified. If one dollar leaves, it must be accounted for in the period that it leaves the organization and no other time. Matching techniques do not work for cost management. With matching techniques, the point when money actually flows can be different from when it is accounted for. Remember how nonsensical the idea of moving water flow was? These accounting techniques allow similar transactions to occur. Although matching is allowed for in financial accounting, when it is used for management decision making, artificial ties are created that limit the organization's ability to function effectively.

Importance of Time

The second important issue to consider when using explicit profit dynamics is time. As we all know, time is one-dimensional and flows in one direction. From a business perspective, we cannot change time, and we must accept it as it exists. Through synchronizing our watches and clocks, we can agree on when things happen. For example, at 8:00 A.M. Eastern, 7:00 A.M. Central, and 5:00 A.M. Pacific, witnesses saw John come to work. Similarly, with revenue flows and total cost flows, we know when the transactions happen. There is no question when a payment is made or received. This is a critical concept, for relativity does not apply when it comes to money. Thirty days is thirty days to all observers. With business, it is all about absolute time.

When it comes to managing a business, time is the most misunderstood concept for two reasons. First, part of the confusion centers on what financial accounting allows from a transactional perspective. The rest of the confusion results from allocating costs and creating false cost flows, resulting in belief of the "time is money" philosophy.

Financial accounting allows some transactions to be reported at a time different from when they actually occurred. This in and of itself is a nonissue from the cost management perspective. When an organization reports something to the government should not be a concern to those who are responsible for managing costs; however, it is a concern to those reporting costs. Since the tools and techniques allowed for financial accounting do not have to reflect reality in its entirety, the financial community should have the responsibility to use the data to make the organization appeal to investors. The problem is the influence of financial accounting on cost or management accounting. Using financial techniques such as accrual methods to manage departments or businesses gives decision makers a false impression of the cost dynamics of the situation. Additionally, financial accounting techniques such as depreciation, which may be considered while justifying the purchase of equipment, apply directly only during the financial accounting process. Machine depreciation itself does not show up on the bottom line although the financial accounting transaction might affect money flow. Once the organization pays for the equipment, the cost is sunk. The organization can choose to sell the machine, but the dollars show up only when this transaction occurs.

The other confusion occurs when allocating costs. Take the concept "time is money," for example. What is the application in an organizational setting? Consider the following example. An organization has one worker making $20.00 per hour. On an average day, this worker should be able to make 20 units, leading to an allocated cost of $1.00 per unit. If the worker has a slow day and averages 15 units per hour, the resulting allocated cost is $1.33. If, however, the worker has a fantastic day and averages 30 units per hour, the allocated unit cost is $0.67. As shown in Exhibit 4.11, the more time that it takes for each unit, the more expensive the allocated unit cost. This would lead to the conclusion that more time means more money and less time means less money and, thus, the belief that "time is money."

The reality of the situation is that total costs remain the same. No additional money has left the organization through the C-R Border. Management did not lower the worker's salary for increased productivity. In fact, it would seem to make more sense that if any salary changes were to be made, the worker's wages would increase. The fact of the matter is the labor cost remains the same in each scenario. The illusion that time is money is directly supported by the allocation process. In reality, however, time does not always mean money.

Exhibit 4.11 Allocating Resources via Time Creates the Impression That Time Is Money

Units	Allocated Unit Cost	Average Time per Unit
15	$1.33	2
20	$1.00	1.5
30	$0.67	1

Dynamics of Cash

The model created with the C-R Border suggests that profit is determined by considering all dollars entering and leaving the organization during a specific point in time. When no time dimension is added, the essential measure focuses on cash rather than profit. Profit is a snapshot of the organization's financial performance. For a given period, the organization's profit was X. Cash, however, is the level in the model that represents how much money the organization has. Being a level, cash can show not only the status of the organization at a particular moment in time, but also when tracked, it can create a picture of performance over time. Snapshots are important, but sometimes a representation over time is a better indicator of how well the organization is performing and how well leaders are managing the organization.

In the end, an organization wants money more so than profit. Profit leads to more money—the immediate proof is found in personal finances. People are more interested in having money in their pockets, in the bank, or in revenue-generating investments than they are interested in the difference between what they make (revenue) and what they pay on a monthly basis (cost). By maximizing the difference, or personal profit, the result is more money.

The intention of the discussion at this point is not to use cash to determine how well the organization is performing. Rather, it is simply an introduction to the fundamentals of profit dynamics. Cash is a measure that represents a state of the organization's finances. The desire is to make decisions that increase profitability. By increasing profitability, the organization improves its cash position.

Since cash is the level for the organization, it becomes the center of the system dynamics equations applied to the organization. The fundamental equations begin with the level equation for the organization. The cash of the organization for a new period is equal to the cash from the previous period added to the profit from the new period (Equation 4.6). This should make intuitive sense. It is equivalent to saying that the new water level in the sink is equal to the previous level of water added to the net flow rate.

$$\text{Cash}_{\text{Current}} = \text{Cash}_{\text{Previous}} + \text{Revenue}_{\text{Current}} - \text{Total Cost}_{\text{Current}} \qquad (4.6)$$

Assume that at some point in time, time 0, the cash of an organization is known. This point will be considered $\text{Cash}_{t=0}$, which represents the cash at time 0. From this point, the cash of the organization at any given time can be determined by using the system dynamics equations and by building on the known information. Projecting cash into the future at some point in time, which we will call time 1 ($Cash_{t=1}$), involves knowing the profit for the period time 1 (Equation 4.7). Since time 1 is arbitrary, it may represent a month, two months, or one year. Equation 4.7 is the equation used to determine the cash at time 1.

$$Cash_{t=1} = Cash_{t=0} + Revenue_{t=1} - Total\ Cost_{t=1} \quad (4.7)$$

Consider a model where cost and revenue information is modeled for a mock company (Exhibit 4.12). Each month in Exhibit 4.13 shows how the revenues and total costs come together to determine profits. The profits created by the revenues and total costs determine the cash (Exhibit 4.14). Changes in profit for a given period affect

Exhibit 4.12   Cost as a Level Is Affected by the Revenue Rate and the Cost Rate

Time	Available Money	Revenue Rate	Cost Rate	Profit
0	$100			
1	$103	$ 21	$ 18	$ 3
2	$101	$ 20	$ 22	$ -2
3	$ 97	$ 19	$ 23	$ -4
Quarter 1	**$ 97**	**$ 60**	**$ 63**	**$ -3**
4	$ 98	$ 19	$ 18	$ 1
5	$100	$ 20	$ 18	$ 2
6	$ 95	$ 20	$ 25	$ -5
Quarter 2	**$ 95**	**$ 59**	**$ 61**	**$ -2**
7	$ 92	$ 21	$ 24	$ -3
8	$ 98	$ 23	$ 17	$ 6
9	$105	$ 24	$ 17	$ 7
Quarter 3	**$105**	**$ 68**	**$ 58**	**$10**
10	$105	$ 22	$ 22	$ 0
11	$115	$ 29	$ 19	$10
12	$126	$ 28	$ 17	$11
Quarter 4	**$126**	**$ 79**	**$ 58**	**$21**
Year	**$126**	**$266**	**$240**	**$26**

Exhibit 4.13   Profits, Revenues, and Costs

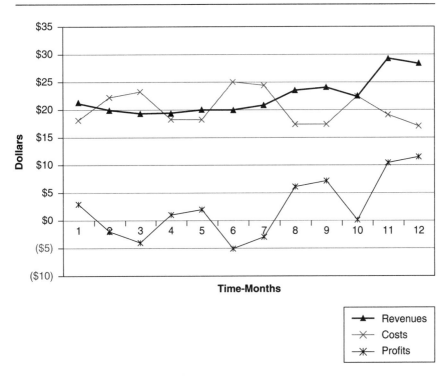

the rate and magnitude of the change to cash, which is represented in tabular form in Exhibit 4.15.

As discussed previously, the way to determine cash in the future is to start with a known amount of cash. Time 0 serves as a reference point for cash in this example. Time 0 might represent, for instance, the amount of cash available after the end of the previous financial year. However, it is just an arbitrary point in time.

From a total cost perspective, each time period represented in Exhibit 4.12 is independent. What happens during any arbitrary time period happens only during that period and does not directly influence what happens in subsequent periods. Management actions and cost levels create the ties between periods. For instance, periods 2 and 3 can be combined to create a larger analysis period. The results from period 2 also can be used to make management changes to increase performance in period 3. What caused the costs may create dependencies, but merely incurring the costs does not force dependence.

Exhibit 4.14   Cash Flow Dynamics

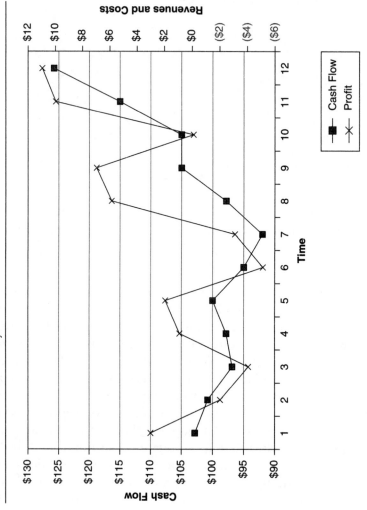

Exhibit 4.15   Only the Profit within a Period Affects Cash

Time	Available Money	Profit	Change in Profit
0	$100		
1	$103	$ 3	$ 0
2	$101	$-2	$-5
3	$ 97	$-4	$-2
4	$ 98	$ 1	$ 5
5	$100	$ 2	$ 1
6	$ 95	$-5	$-7
7	$ 92	$-3	$ 2
8	$ 98	$ 6	$ 9
9	$105	$ 7	$ 1
10	$105	$ 0	$-7
11	$115	$10	$10
12	$126	$11	$ 1

Profits for an arbitrary period j, then, cannot be determined by costs that occurred in a period before j. The profits can be *influenced* by the activities that occurred in periods $j - 1$ and before, such as when an organization designs a product in 2001 and begins selling it in 2002.

One problem with cost accounting is that it does not holistically follow the law of conservation of dollars. Although activities occurred and salaries were paid during period j, companies have the option to move costs from period to period, thus violating the law of conservation of dollars. Where dollars are moved from one period to another to determine the profitability of that being analyzed, matching principles are at fault. The movement of dollars is a direct violation of the law of conservation of dollars. In principle, it is similar to moving water flow across periods either before or after it was incurred.

If the amount of money an organization has in a given period is considered, the magnitude can only change in two ways: either revenue is received or expenses are paid. If a large enough period is chosen, it is often assumed that both costs and revenues will be accounted for. However, this is not always the case. In most cases, it is possible to identify costs that were incurred prior to the beginning of the analysis period that can be tied to revenue flows that occurred during the analysis period. In cases where revenues and costs occur in different periods, something interesting happens. Usually costs will occur before revenues, although this is not always the case (for example, up-front payments). Assume costs are incurred in period ϵ_i and revenues are received in period ϵ_j, where $i < j$. This implies that when the revenues are received, the *costs* involved in generating the revenues are actually *sunk costs*, or nonrecoverable costs. There is nothing the organization can do about decreasing or changing these costs. The issue, then, becomes how an organization can generate the most profit given the fact that development costs, manufacturing costs, and all other associated costs have already occurred. The emphasis of management should shift away from accounting for costs and toward managing costs and maximizing revenues during the current period.

Management decisions should focus on the increased true profitability of the organization. The profitability measure should be as objective as possible to eliminate any ambiguity regarding the effect decisions have on organization performance. Therefore, given the time dependence of organization performance, the profit equation and its development must be used to get the full effect of decisions and their past or future impact on organization performance.

When making management decisions, however, costs should not be considered independently of revenues. Decisions should reflect the combination of revenue flows and total cost flows for the recent past, current, and future. To make a cost decision without understanding its impact on profit makes no sense. How often has a company laid off resources, for example, only to find that it is constrained to develop, sell, or deliver its products or services? How often have companies chosen not to implement a technology because it would increase costs even though the revenues might increase at an even greater rate?

One important point is that management decisions need to occur in an environment where those making the decisions are thinking about profit and not just costs. There is no assurance that cost reduction alone leads to increased profitability. To reiterate a second point, the level of money only changes for revenues and total costs during the period incurred. Although the statement appears obvious, it is much deeper. Consider a company that chooses to perform research and to develop a new product for market. First, assume that the researcher's cost is fixed. Therefore, regardless of what ideas the researcher develops or fails to develop, the total cost to the organization is the same. This raises another important point: there really is limited change in organizational cost to perform research if most of the costs are resource costs. Of course, action and item costs may exist. For example, assume that an American automobile company purchases a German car from a competitor and chooses to disassemble the car to reverse engineer it. The cost of the engineers who will do the evaluation is a resource cost and is therefore fixed. The trip to Germany and the price of the car both can be considered costs associated with the research. If the research work occurs in the year 2001, it is not likely that the company will get much benefit from the work until sometime into the future, such as the year 2003.

How is this situation to be interpreted in an explicit profit dynamics environment? It is simple. The organization incurs the costs in 2001 and the revenues beginning in 2003. The cost and revenue flows are independent, for the company has multiple options. It can choose not to do anything with the research, as most companies that do research work have experienced. If the company does nothing with the research, the result will be no new products from which the company would receive revenues. The organization also can choose to make products with the results of the research, which can lead to revenue-generating opportunities for the company sometime in the future. These revenue-generating opportunities can vary. For example, the company might choose to put the technology into one product, it might choose to put it in all products, or politics might cause the organization to put the technology in some but not all of the products. The organization might also decide to sell the technology to someone else, or it might choose to license the technology. Whatever the company chooses to do in the future, it has already paid the price for the research; the research is a sunk cost. The profit of the organization is determined at the time of the research—in 2001.

The purpose of the research is to help the company position itself for future revenues, profits, and cash, which is really all that it does from a profit perspective. Product research and development serves the purpose to develop products and services that sometime in the future will offset research and development for future products. Therefore, the research and development costs today should be tied to the revenues generated from products designed yesterday.

The effects of this can be seen in Exhibit 4.13. For the first six months, the total costs are generally higher. For the first quarter, or three-month period, the total costs are $63.00 ($18.00 + $22.00 + $23.00), while for the second quarter they are $61.00 ($18.00 + $18.00 + $25.00). For this discussion, assume that these higher total costs represent additional work used to develop new products that the organization will sell during the latter two quarters. The revenues that determine the profit for the first two quarters likely are generated from products developed sometime in the past. The pricing schema, therefore, should focus on offsetting current total costs or total costs anticipated over a certain period rather than extending out sometime into the future and tying them to the product. This concept is developed further in Chapter 5.

Companies, however, tend to tie the costs of development to the revenues associated with the resulting products. This results in measures such as the life-cycle cost of a product. The intention often is to determine the total cost to a company for much, if not all, of the life of a product. If the company knows the product life-cycle costs, the break-even price is calculable. Although the intention is good, from an explicit profit dynamics perspective, it leads to decisions that suboptimize the organization's behavior.

Organizations often assume that when they place a new product on the market, they should price the product to recover the design and development costs. However, the design costs from an explicit cost dynamics perspective are sunk costs. Pricing products to recover something that is already gone makes little sense. This practice limits organizations from effectively pricing their products and from making strong marketing moves by cannibalizing their products.

Organizations often price their products in one of two ways. The first is to determine how much it costs to make the product and then to determine the price by adding a profit margin on top of the cost. Therefore, if the product is believed to cost $10.00, the selling price might be $11.50 if the organization desires a 15 percent profit margin. The second way that companies determine price is through value. Often organizations accept market price to reflect the market value of their products. Organizations get into trouble when they try to price in order to recover development costs.

The first method of pricing, where the company adds a margin to its product, is one of the most common situations. Assume that the company has a new technology on which it has spent millions of dollars developing. Companies such as this will determine the total development costs of the product and usually will apply an allocation technique to determine a development cost per product. By adding a profit margin to this cost, a price is derived. This is one reason why many new drugs are so expensive. Companies in this position may unnecessarily price themselves out of certain markets because of the assumption that they must recover the development costs. These development costs, however, are often long gone by the time the product hits the market. The objective therefore would be to price today's products so that they can sustain today's research for tomorrow's products.

The second pricing scenario involves value-based pricing and is tied to the first scenario. Assume, for instance, that the organization wants to sell the $11.50 item mentioned previously in a new market. Recall that the cost to develop and make the products supposedly was $10.00. If the market price for the product is too low, some companies choose to get out of the business because their margins are too low. They forget, perhaps, that they need revenue from these products to support research and development for future products and services. By understanding the profit dynamics, organizations have more flexibility in pricing given the inevitable changes in market value for the products, they may realize that they can actually price below $10 and make money. Chapter 8 includes more discussion regarding pricing practices.

From this analysis, it is possible to begin to understand relationships between costs, revenues, and profits, all from the objective perspective provided by the profit dynamics model. This information forms the basis for the law of conservation of dollars. Two very important assumptions are made that, along with the development just discussed, make up the basis for explicit profit dynamics:

1. Time naturally occurs along a continuum. Violation of this continuum by moving dollar flows into periods when they did not occur for management purposes leads to profitability and cash on paper that are different from the true profitability and cash. This is a critical point, for the decisions that are believed to lead to a desired result can lead to a different result.

2. When observing the performance of a business over time, arguably the most important measure is profit. Profit leads to more money for the organization. To determine an organization's profitability, revenues and costs incurred over a period are considered. When making profit-oriented decisions, revenues and costs must be considered together. One of the most important issues regarding the determination of financial performance is time. What is of interest is what flows into and out of the C-R Border over the analysis period in question. Adherence to the principles that are really common sense will ultimately lead to increased profitability.

Endnotes

[1]Eliyahu M. Goldratt and Jeff Cox, *The Goal: A Process of Ongoing Improvement,* 2nd ed. (Croton-on-Hudson, NY: North River Press, 1992).

[2]Jay W. Forrester, *Principles of Systems* (Cambridge, MA: The MIT Press, 1968), pp. 1–7.

[3]Peter M. Senge, *The Fifth Discipline: The Art & Practice of the Learning Organization* (New York: Doubleday Currency, 1990).

5

Basic Explicit Cost Dynamics Measures

Up to this point, the emphasis has been on understanding cost and revenue flows. This chapter will introduce the basic measures used with explicit cost dynamics (ECD). Because it is important for the reader to understand how the measures were derived, this is one of the more mathematically focused chapters. In every case, the measure has direct ties to the bottom line so that the practitioner will know each action's direct bottom-line impact (BLI). In the development of ECD and the measures used, maintaining integrity or direct ties to the bottom line were important. In this manner, no ambiguity will show up in the formulae, scope, description, and use. Two more very important concepts are introduced in this chapter. First is the unit cost uncertainty property, which states the limitations associated with trying to determine a unit cost. Second is the idea of a double break-even point.

Allocation-based costing can be used to determine a cost per unit. For example, assume it costs $1,000.00 to set up a machine. If 1,000 units were made, the allocated cost would be $1.00 per unit. If the production were 100 instead of 1,000, the setup cost would be $10.00 per unit. If one unit were produced, the one unit would assume all of the cost. As extremes are approached, interesting results occur. What would happen if the organization made an infinite number of units? The setup costs would go away and no cost would be allocated. What if someone set up the machine but decided not to make any of the products? Would the setup cost now be infinite? Have you ever wondered why it is so difficult to determine the cost of

Exhibit 5.1   Direct Labor Cost Is Determined by Considering the Rate of Production (Hours/Unit) and the Cost of Direct Labor ($/Hour)

Product	Machine Time Minutes/Unit	Direct Labor	Direct Labor Cost
A	30	$30	$15
B	10	$30	$ 5

a unit of production? Why are examples such as the one just described, which are not valid in all cases, allowed to dominate our decision making?

Perhaps the cost of a product really does not exist. The same person on different days might get a different cost per unit of a product. Different techniques get different answers; even the same techniques get different answers. With there being so many different ways to try to get the same answer and with each way determining a different answer, the logical conclusion is that the cost of a product cannot be determined.

To get a unit cost in the traditional sense of the phrase, an organization must allocate costs. Consider the following three examples:

1. *The traditional approach.* The organization chooses to allocate indirect costs or overhead costs based on machine hours.

2. *The progressive approach.* The company realizes that materials are a much greater percentage of the cost of a unit than direct labor, so it decides to allocate based on material costs.

3. *The activity-based costing (ABC) approach.* This organization decides to allocate indirect labor based on the percentage of time that indirect laborers spend on each product.

To compare techniques, the direct labor is assumed to be constant as is the material cost in each scenario. The direct labor costs can be seen in Exhibit 5.1.

TRADITIONAL APPROACH

The organization chooses to determine the cost of a unit by allocating indirect hours using machine hours as a basis. As most readers are aware, this method of allocation has been in existence since the beginning of cost accounting. At one point in time, direct labor was

Exhibit 5.2   Scenario 1 Involves Allocating Based on Machine Time

Product	Machine Hours	Percent of Total Hours	Indirect Labor	Allocated
A	30	75	$1,000	$750
B	10	25	$1,000	$250

such a large percentage of the cost of a product that allocating indirect labor using machine hours drew no questions. The organization allocated 5 percent of a cost (indirect) based on the 95 percent portion (direct). This seemed like a harmless approach.

To determine the direct labor cost, companies will usually multiply the direct labor rate ($/hour) by the machine time for a unit (hour/unit). To determine the indirect cost, if the organization only produces the two products, the machine time for Product A is three times that for Product B. Therefore, according to this logic, Product A should get three times the allocated indirect labor cost (Exhibit 5.2).

PROGRESSIVE APPROACH

The organization using the progressive approach realizes that it no longer makes sense to allocate indirect costs based on machine hours. Now, material costs comprise much more of the unit cost of a product than direct labor hours. In this case, for Product A, the material cost is $200.00 while the direct labor is $15.00. For Product B, the material cost is $100.00 while the direct labor cost is $5.00. To reflect its view of reality, the organization has chosen to allocate based on material costs rather than labor costs.

The approach is similar to the traditional approach where more money is allocated to the product with more material costs. Since the material costs are twice the cost for Product A than they are for Product B, twice the indirect labor will be applied to Product A than to Product B (Exhibit 5.3).

Exhibit 5.3   Scenario 2 Involves Allocating Based on Material Costs

Product	Material Costs	Percent of Total Materials	Indirect Labor	Allocated
A	200	67	$1,000	$667
B	100	33	$1,000	$333

ACTIVITY-BASED COSTING APPROACH

Something still does not seem right to the organization. Consultants have just presented a report suggesting that although the material and direct labor costs are correct, the indirect labor allocations are incorrect. After performing a study, the consultants concluded that, in general, the pool of indirect labor spends four times more of its time on Product B than it does on Product A (Exhibit 5.4). To allocate based on material costs does not make sense either. Material costs have nothing to do with how indirect labor spends its time. Therefore, the right approach is for Product B to carry four times the cost from the indirect labor pool. Now, the consultants suggest, the company knows exactly how much it costs to make Product A and Product B.

WHO IS RIGHT?

Exhibits 5.5 and 5.6 show the resulting cost numbers. If it were your organization, which cost would you choose? Assume that you have to pick one. The numbers are so different, how would you know what selling price you would use for your product? If someone offered you

Exhibit 5.4   Scenario 3 Uses Activity-Based Costing as Its Allocation Method

Product	Percent of Indirect Time Spent	Indirect Labor	Allocated
A	20	$1,000	$200
B	80	$1,000	$800

Exhibit 5.5   With Differing Techniques and Assumptions, Determining a Unit Cost for Product A Is Impossible

Product A	Material	Direct Labor	Allocated	Cost per Unit
Scenario 1	200	15	$750	$965
Scenario 2	200	15	$667	$882
Scenario 3	200	15	$200	$415

Exhibit 5.6 With Differing Techniques and Assumptions,
            Determining a Unit Cost for Product B Is Impossible

Product B	Material	Direct Labor	Allocated	Cost per Unit
Scenario 1	100	5	$250	$355
Scenario 2	100	5	$333	$438
Scenario 3	100	5	$800	$905

$700.00 for one unit of Product A, would you accept? Why or why not? How about $600.00 for Product B?

Note that in all three scenarios for each product, the cost dynamics remain the same. The material costs are the same, the labor costs are the same, and the indirect labor is the same. Allocating creates confusion because so many allocating techniques can be used. Each allocation, however, is actually arbitrary. Although ABC seems more logical, what makes it more desirable to some than the other techniques is its more compelling argument. With ABC, the corporation will examine exactly how the pool being allocated spends its time to figure out how much should be applied to which product. However, the technique is still arbitrary, and it still does not work. In its technique and use, ABC is no different from allocating based on machine hours, material costs, or the number of blue versus black trucks that drive by the front of the building.

ALLOCATION

As mentioned before, the cost dynamics in each of these situations remains the same. It cannot be argued that a check for $100.00 was written during a given period for the purchase of materials. However, whether a unit of production costs $355.00, $438.00, or $905.00 can be questioned. Allocation techniques, which attempt to attach certain types of overhead to the unit cost of a product, have inherent problems. Such techniques try to change the true nature of these costs. The nature of overhead is that of a resource cost, which is independent of the number of units produced, and that nature cannot be changed without expecting discrepancies between what the technique suggests and what actually happens. Even if the most accurate measuring devices and techniques were used to determine cost, the fact remains that variances will still exist because the cost types are naturally different and independent.

Companies might attempt to argue that the overhead costs allocated using ABC are not independent of units produced. The proof that they are is simple. If the company chooses not to make any products, would the costs go away? No—the costs would exist until someone took the step to eliminate them (discussed in Chapter 6). The company also can choose to keep the cost and have the employees do something else. What about the fact that the technique is arbitrary? An organization can allocate by hours, for example, or by actual costs of labor being used (fewer hours spent by more expensive resources can change the ratios used in scenario 3). Which is correct? If by hours, how does a company allocate the unproductive hours? If by labor costs, how does the company ensure the relationship between value added and labor costs? One product might be more expensive because labor resources with more seniority are working on it even though they may not be putting in as many hours of work as the newer employees with less experience. There will always be an argument against each allocation technique because these techniques are arbitrary.

Why do companies allocate? Ultimately, they want to know how much a unit of something costs. When the organization knows how much the unit costs, it will know whether the current price determined by the market is profitable or not. From a cost management perspective, it is that simple. Companies do not allocate for allocation's sake. They are attempting to get useful information so that better decisions can be made. Clearly, for financial accounting purposes, allocating helps keep track of information such as the value that is added to inventory for reporting purposes. However, this exercise is really of limited, if any, use when managing costs.

CAN THE UNIT PRICE BE DETERMINED?

Regardless of the technique or the detail, no one can determine the unit cost of a product in the traditional sense. In fact, the unit cost of a product does not exist. This is the unit cost uncertainty hypothesis. The traditional sense involves taking much of the cost of a company—its labor—and applying it to something that varies for many different reasons. An organization cannot determine the allocated cost of an item. Because the techniques necessary to get to this level of detail are arbitrary, an organization can never be sure that its technique is less arbitrary than another. It is like the saying, "The person with one watch always knows the time. The person with two watches is never sure."

Additionally, some of the cost inputs do not behave as once believed. For example, material costs are typically a given in terms of calculating the cost of a product. Materials, however, are not necessarily a given in terms of the cost of a product. As will be discussed in detail in Chapter 7, material costs can either be tied to the organization or tied to the product or service. If materials cannot directly be allocated to a product, how does an organization determine what it costs to make a product?

Because a company cannot determine the allocated cost does not mean that management information, cost information, and pricing information cannot be captured and used. In fact, ECD offers more accurate and useful information than traditional systems. The information that ECD offers reflects actual cost and revenue dynamics while adhering to the law of conservation of dollars and the unit cost uncertainty hypothesis.

OBJECTIVE OF COST MANAGEMENT

Cost management and cost management systems have two objectives. The first objective is to help the organization to manage its operations and to keep costs at a reasonable level. This involves understanding the types of costs that exist and how and why organizations incur them. The second reason is to provide information to help the organization understand what its revenues must be to ensure profitability.

To help the organization keep costs at a reasonable level, managers must have a good understanding of the cost dynamics, the cost levels, and the right measures. It is important to know that the decisions that are made have a BLI. Few things are worse to a manager than to approve a project that promises millions in savings only to not see it materialize on the bottom line. Recall, for example, cost-justification exercises where increasing the productivity of an engineer paid $50,000.00 per year by 10 percent leads to a savings of $5,000.00 per year. Obviously, managers should not rely on any cost management and project-justification tools that allow for such suggestions.

To provide information for pricing, the cost management system must give managers a clear picture of the cost dynamics so that they can ensure that the pricing will recover the resource costs. By knowing the exact cost position, value pricing and strategic pricing can come together to ensure the highest profitability for the organization. More detail regarding pricing strategy will follow in Chapter 8.

Through its measures, ECD provides real-time cost information. Since they are all derived from the bottom line, the manager knows what the costs are at any time. Additionally, with the option to view cost levels and cost types, managers have even more relevant details regarding bottom-line costs. With the tools developed later in the chapter, pricing, although slightly more complicated, ensures that those doing the pricing will have the desired impact on the bottom line.

EXPLICIT COST DYNAMICS MEASURES

Chapter 3 introduced the concept cost types, which include resource costs, action costs, and item costs. From a total cost perspective, by adding all of the costs that the organization incurs over a period, the total cost for that period would be derived (Equation 5.1).

$$\text{Total Cost} = \Sigma \text{ Cost Types} \tag{5.1}$$

This action would include adding all of the resource costs in the period as well as the action and item costs (Equation 5.2). In addition, the costs being analyzed for the period in question must only happen during the period in question.

$$\text{Total Cost} = \Sigma \text{ Resource Costs} + \Sigma \text{ Action Costs} + \Sigma \text{ Item Costs} \tag{5.2}$$

Similarly, by adding all of the costs within the cost levels within the organization, the same value for the total cost can be found (Equation 5.3). Recall that cost levels organize the cost types into groups based on how and why the costs were incurred. To recap, the levels are the program level, the superprogram level, and the resource level (Equation 5.4). By identifying each of these within a period and summing them, the total cost for that period should be determined.

$$\text{Total Cost} = \Sigma \text{ Cost Levels} \tag{5.3}$$

$$\text{Total Cost} = \Sigma \text{ Resource Costs} + \Sigma \text{ Superprogram Costs} + \Sigma \text{ Program Costs} \tag{5.4}$$

Each cost type must exist within a cost level. If, for example, an organization incurs a cost within a certain period, the reason for incurring the cost will exist within the definition or scope of the program within the particular cost level. Since all programs are made up of cost types and all programs must fit within a cost level, the integrity between cost levels and the programs that create the cost is maintained.

When it comes to ECD (and, in general), total cost *is* total cost; there is no ambiguity with these concepts. It can be correctly assumed, therefore, that with integrity between cost levels and cost types maintained, the sum of the action costs and the item costs must equal the sum of the program and superprogram costs (Equation 5.5). In other words, the item and action costs comprise the program costs and the superprogram costs. The program will not have its own resource costs, and neither will the superprogram. What will identify the program and the superprogram from a cost perspective are the actions and the items that are specific to a program.

$$\Sigma \text{ Action Costs} + \Sigma \text{ Item Cost} = \Sigma \text{ Program Costs}$$
$$+ \Sigma \text{ Superprogram Costs} \qquad (5.5)$$

To determine the total program and superprogram costs, simply add the actions and the items associated with all programs that occur within the analysis period (Equation 5.6). For a specific program, identify the specific actions and items associated with that program. For example, a consulting program that is doing work for client X might incur costs associated with travel and lodging (action costs) as well as having to buy computers and particular software (item costs). If the company incurs these costs within the same period, they would be summed using Equation 5.7 to determine the cost of this specific program—consulting for client X.

$$\text{Total Program Cost} = \sum_{\text{All Programs}} \text{Actions Costs} + \sum_{\text{All Programs}} \text{Item Costs} \qquad (5.6)$$

$$\text{Specific Program Cost} = \Sigma \text{ Actions Costs}_{\text{Specific Program}}$$
$$+ \Sigma \text{ Item Costs}_{\text{Specific Program}} \qquad (5.7)$$

In general, there are two types of programs and superprograms: internally facing (IF) and externally facing (EF). The IF programs are responsible for operating the organization and preparing it for future activities, and their main purpose is to maintain and improve the operations of the organization. By definition, these programs do not generate revenue. Thus, all operations and processes associated with operating the organization are IF programs. How an IF program is defined is determined by the organization. It may choose to define departments as IF programs, for example, or it may choose to define cross-functional processes as IF programs. Deciding how an organization should define its programs is beyond the scope of this chapter.

Since IF programs focus on organizational issues, they comprise part of the total operating costs of the organization. The other part is the resource cost. When the IF program costs are summed with the resource costs over a period, the result is the total organization operating cost, or *org cost* (Equation 5.8). These cost functions are multidimensional in nature and exist as a result of operating the company. The program portions of org cost can vary linearly, while the resource portion changes in steps (see Chapter 2).

$$\text{Organization Operating Cost} =$$
$$\text{Resource Costs} + \Sigma \text{Superprograms}_{IF} + \Sigma \text{Programs}_{IF} \qquad (5.8)$$

By contrast, EF programs exist for the sole purpose of generating revenue for the organization. This may involve the producing and selling of goods and services. They are customer facing in that they allow the organization to interact with existing and future customers to sell the organization's goods. It is important to note that EF programs do not refer to the infrastructure to produce and sell; rather, the people and much of the infrastructure are org costs. The programs themselves are used to sell the goods that make up the EF program. For example, the process to fill a customer order would be an EF program. When the customer places an order with the organization, the organization incurs costs to fill this order. If, for example, the organization operates as a build-to-order firm, the costs incurred are those associated with procuring the materials, the materials and utilities associated with producing the order, and shipping the order. The costs incurred that are necessary only to fill the order are those associated with EF programs. The costs associated with EF programs are called customer operating costs, or CO costs. To determine the CO cost total for a period, simply sum the program and superprogram costs that are related to generating revenues over the period (Equation 5.9).

$$\text{CO Cost} = \Sigma \text{Superprograms}_{EF} + \Sigma \text{Programs}_{EF} \qquad (5.9)$$

The total cost for a period now can be defined in many ways, all of which lead to the same value. The organization can sum all of the resource costs, action costs, and item costs to determine a value for total cost. This approach is useful when the cost type is the view of the cost data that the organization desires. The organization can look at cost levels to determine total costs, which allows it to have a cost view across programs and superprograms. Finally, customer operating costs and organization costs can be summed to get a view of how these costs break down (Equation 5.10). Chapter 8 will focus on managing these costs in organizations and how to make profitable decisions given their existence.

$$\text{Total Cost} = \Sigma \text{ CO Costs} + \Sigma \text{ organization Cost} \qquad (5.10)$$

COST RECOVERY RATIO

As stated previously, the objective is not to manage or to reduce costs. The objective is to be profitable. The purpose of this section is to introduce measures that will help organizations understand what is profitable behavior and what is not. The section begins with the profit equation and develops the subsequent measures based on this equation. This development shows that the integrity of each of the equations with the profit equation is maintained.

The bottom-line profit equation is the only equation that measures ultimate profitability (Equation 5.11). Since it alone calculates profitability, all measures should tie directly to this equation so that those making decisions have an immediate understanding of the BLI of their decision. Therefore, the development of measures starts with this equation.

$$\text{Profit} = \Sigma \text{Revenues}_{\text{Period}} - \Sigma \text{Total Costs}_{\text{Period}} \qquad (5.11)$$

Begin by assuming that there is no loss and no profit, a condition commonly known as breakeven (or, as used in the equations, BE). At breakeven, the revenues are equal to the costs (Equation 5.12). Profit is equal to zero. By setting the costs and the revenues equal to each other, the equation can be manipulated using simple algebra. Substituting Equation 5.10 into Equation 5.12 creates a new description for the total cost portion of the equation (Equation 5.13). This equation simply states that at breakeven the revenues must equal the sum of the CO costs and the org costs.

$$\Sigma \text{Revenue}_{\text{BE}} = \Sigma \text{Total Cost}_{\text{BE}} \qquad (5.12)$$

$$\Sigma \text{Revenue}_{\text{BE}} = \Sigma \text{ CO Costs}_{\text{BE}} + \Sigma \text{ Organization Operating Cost}_{\text{BE}} \qquad (5.13)$$

Continuing with the algebra, subtracting CO costs from both sides leads to Equation 5.14. The terms on each side of this equation are worth discussing. The term on the left side of the equation makes an interesting statement. Remember that CO costs generate the revenue for the organization. Therefore, the term on the left side of the equation suggests that the revenues generated by the activities must exceed the CO costs by an amount equal to the org cost for the company to break even. In other words, the organization must ensure this difference in its revenue-generating activities in order to at least break even. When it comes to pricing, the important objective is to generate revenues—enough revenues to offset the org costs for the current period and the CO costs generated while creating and selling the goods or services. In reality, this is the same information that an organization looks for when allocating costs. The ultimate objective is to ensure that sales are large enough to recover operating or org costs. Through decoupling the selling price options from the costs, this approach offers the organization much more flexibility in terms of its pricing.

$$\text{Revenue} - \text{CO Costs} = \text{Organization Operating Costs} \quad (5.14)$$

Continuing this thought, if both sides of the equation were divided by the org costs, the result is a ratio that is the key to managing and pricing goods and services (Equation 5.15). The numerator of the equation is referred to as the program margin. The ratio itself is the cost recovery ratio (CRR). When the ratio is equal to one, the organization is at its overall break-even point. When the ratio is greater than one, the numerator is greater than the denominator, which means that the organization is operating at a profit.

$$\frac{\Sigma \text{Revenue} - \Sigma \text{CO Costs}}{\Sigma \text{Organization Operating Costs}} = 1 \quad (5.15)$$

PROGRAM MARGIN

The purpose of the program margin (or PM, as used in the equations), which applies to EF programs, is to provide guidance in terms of what opportunities the organization has from a pricing perspective. As shown in Equation 5.16, when the program margin is positive, the program itself has made money and will therefore contribute to paying off the org costs. Just how much it contributes to reducing the org costs depends on the difference between the revenues and the CO costs.

$$PM = Revenue_{\text{Specific Program}} - Costs_{\text{Specific Program}} \quad (5.16)$$

To ensure that the program pays the org costs, the program must be profitable itself (Exhibit 5.7). Therefore, when pricing goods and services, the costs associated with creating and selling must be covered with the pricing (Equation 5.17). Those involved with managing the program must either raise revenues or reduce costs to ensure that the program margin is positive. If the program margin is equal to zero, the program breaks even and is therefore incapable of paying off the org costs. The organization may or may not be better off in this scenario. It may, for example, gain valuable experience that can help with future work without having an adverse effect on the cost side of the profit equation.

$$PM = Revenue_{EF} - (\Sigma\, Action\ Costs_{EF} - \Sigma\, Item\ Costs_{EF}) \quad (5.17)$$

The worse case is when the organization takes on work that causes it to be worse off than it would have been had it not created and performed the activities associated with the program. The organization must have very important tactical and strategic reasons for taking on this type of work.

The CRR allows organizations to immediately see how they are performing financially and, at any given point in time, how far they must go to achieve profitability. It also can be a mechanism to measure and compare programs. One activity, for instance, might be to determine and compare CRRs of various projects. The CRR for a project would just be the ratio of the program margin and the organization costs.

$$CRR = \frac{PM}{Organization\ Operating\ Cost} \quad (5.18)$$

Exhibit 5.7   The Program Margin Determines the Profitability of the Program

Program Margin	Meaning
<0	Program is unprofitable
0	Program breaks even
>0	Program is profitable

CRR =

$$\frac{\text{Revenue}_{\text{Specific Program}} - (\Sigma \text{Action Costs}_{\text{Specific Program}} + \text{Item Costs}_{\text{Specific Program}})}{\text{Organization Operating Cost}} \quad (5.19)$$

The CRR can take on many different values. From Equations 5.18 and 5.19, if the CRR is negative, the program margin is negative, which leads to an unprofitable program. If the CRR is zero, the suggestion is that the program is at breakeven. This is the program break-even point. For values greater than zero and less than one, the numerator is positive but not as large as the denominator. Therefore, the program has broken even but the organization has not. The more traditional break-even point occurs when the CRR is equal to one, which means that all of the costs are offset by all of the revenues. Finally, with a CRR greater than one, the organization is operating as a profitable operation (Exhibit 5.8).

When considering a total cost approach, two break-even points actually exist. The first break-even point provides a milestone for the program and its profitability, while the second provides a milestone for the organization as a whole.

ANSWER TO THE EXAMPLE USING THE ECD APPROACH

Returning to the original problem, at what price should the company sell its products? First, assume that the resource costs are the sum of the direct and indirect labor. These costs are $30.00 per hour, and the indirect costs are $1,000.00 per hour. The total resource costs are $1,030.00 per hour. If the company were to assume that raw materials are not inventoried but are purchased directly for existing customer demand, the materials become the only CO cost. For Product A, with CO costs being $200.00, any sales price above $200.00 will have a positive program margin. Similarly, Product B can be sold for any price above $100.00. At a price of $500.00, Product A has a CRR of approximately 0.29 (Exhibit 5.9). This means that each unit sold at $500.00 recovers 29 percent of the resource costs. To sell three in one hour almost covers the resource costs completely. At a sales price of $500.00, Product B has a CRR of approximately 0.39, meaning that each unit sold at this price covers 39 percent of the resource costs (Exhibit 5.10). If the exact sales price is desired, select the desired CRR and use algebra to determine the price. For example, for a CRR of 0.6 for Product B, the sales price

Exhibit 5.8   There Are Actually Two Break-Even Points to Consider
When Making Profit-Oriented Decisions

Condition	Meaning
CRR < 0	Unprofitable program
CRR = 0	Program breakeven
0 < CRR < 1	Program profitable below traditional breakeven
CRR = 1	Traditional breakeven
CRR > 1	Profitable operation

Exhibit 5.9   Product A and Potential Price Options and Their
Respective CRRs

Resource Cost	CO Cost	Price Product A	CRR
$1,030	$200	$200	0
$1,030	$200	$400	0.18
$1,030	$200	$500	0.29
$1,030	$200	$750	0.53
$1,030	$200	$1,230	1

Exhibit 5.10   Product B and Potential Price Options and Their
Respective CRRs

Resource Cost	CO Cost	Product B Price	CRR
$1,030	$100	$100	0
$1,030	$100	$400	0.29
$1,030	$100	$500	0.39
$1,030	$100	$750	0.63
$1,030	$100	$1,130	1

should be $718.00. Clearly, this approach provides more pricing options for the company and provides more information for each transaction than traditional allocation-based costing systems. (Pricing is covered in more detail in Chapter 8.)

The CRR is different from profit margins. It gives a company a feel for how quickly product or *job* sales recover the fixed costs associated with operating the company. The CRR can be used as a measurement to determine prices or even whether certain programs should be implemented at all. If the total resource costs, the action costs, and the item costs are known and if a predetermined CRR target is established, program margins and, thus, prices can be determined. In the case of bidding on prices, the only unknown might be the price. If all costs are known and the company has a minimum CRR that it would like to meet, the price can be subsequently determined from the CRR.

6

Degree of Freedom Management

Think about whether you ever have been involved—either as the victim or the culprit—in a scenario such as the following: An excited young engineer runs into your office. "The project is a no-brainer. Look at the numbers on this thing. The software costs $300,000.00, and the savings will be 10 times what we paid for the software. We were very conservative with the savings, yet we still come out way ahead. We would be crazy not to do this." So, you approve the budget for the project, fully anticipating that the numbers are, in fact, conservative. Six months after the implementation, no savings are realized. At twelve months, you see some savings but not 10 times what you paid for the software. A full two years pass, and still the savings are not close to what the engineer predicted. What happened?

Although a number of things could have gone wrong, one very common problem is the confidence placed in causal relationships that do not exist; in this case, implementing the software for a price of $300,000.00 will somehow lead to savings of $3,000,000.00. Where did the savings come from? Often, project justifications identify labor improvements, reduction in material and inventory costs, and reduction in transaction costs. However, how real are these cost savings? There are two dynamics at work that suggest that the savings are not always real. The first dynamic is the assumption that things are related when, in fact, they are not. If someone implements software, costs will be reduced. How will costs be reduced? Why will costs be reduced? When will costs be reduced?

What costs will be reduced? How this happens might not totally be clear to those who are justifying the project. The second dynamic centers on whether the cost reductions themselves follow or violate the law of conservation of dollars. Does less money really leave the organization? Can the numbers be verified using explicit cost dynamics (ECD) principles? If they cannot, the validity of the numbers being reported should be questioned.

RELATED ACTIVITIES AND CAUSAL RELATIONSHIPS

Assume that the project team responsible for justifying the implementation of engineering design software identifies labor savings as a result of operating with the new software. Labor savings typically are related to the elimination of unnecessary work or to an increase in productivity. If a worker no longer has to perform a task, the cost of performing that task is assumed to be lower. Companies often assume a productivity increase in situations such as this one. Another type of productivity increase often cited by companies is the increase associated with doing something faster. If a worker can perform a task 10 percent faster, there must be a cost savings associated with it. Will these savings occur? No, not directly. The situations might create the opportunity to reduce costs, but if the cost reductions occur, they do not occur on their own. A direct causal relationship between implementing the software and the resulting cost savings usually does not exist. Achieving the cost reductions as a result of eliminating unnecessary work is a much more complicated situation than it seems.

Begin with the idea of an automobile being assembled. Assume, for the sake of discussion, that a tire installer can install three tires per minute on an assembly line. Thus, the rate is one tire every 20 seconds. An engineer, however, argues that with a new technology on the market, productivity can be increased to one tire every 15 seconds. Since 5 seconds have been taken out of the operating time, a 25 percent improvement in productivity results. If the line operator has a salary of $20.00 per hour, the 25 percent cost reduction translates to $5.00 in savings per hour.

Such a justification for cost reduction is a violation of the law of conservation of dollars. The suggestion is that money can be saved without reducing the amount of money leaving the organization. In

other words, as the situation currently stands, no costs have been reduced, for the laborer still makes the same amount of money per
hour as before. So, if the amount of money spent on labor does not
go down, how can costs be saved? For the organization to be more
profitable as a result of this transaction, it must destroy its own
money. As shown in Equation 6.1, if the net flow rate is zero, the
money in each period must be the same. As mentioned in Chapter 2,
the costs will actually go up because more materials are consumed
and the organization must pay for the new technology. *Thus, if nothing is done after implementing the improved technology, not only will the organization not increase its profit, but also it will possibly be less profitable!*
Without destroying its own money, there is no way that the organization is more profitable in this situation.

$$\text{Money}_j = \text{Money}_{j-1} + \text{Net Flow Rate}_j$$
$$\text{Net Flow Rate}_j \leq 0$$
$$\text{Money}_j \leq \text{Money}_{j+1} \tag{6.1}$$

Does this mean that companies should not improve? No, it does
not mean that at all. What it suggests is that we need to identify, measure, and track decisions in a way that more effectively reflects the
ECD of the situation. In other words, we must understand what the
technology or process improvement will change. In reference to
the scenario just discussed, for example, increasing the production
enables managers to increase their options, or their degrees of freedom for decision making.

DEGREE OF FREEDOM MANAGEMENT

The concept of a degree of freedom when managing an organization
is very important. By focusing on degrees of freedom, it is possible to
identify why something may occur, to recognize the causal relationships between actions or activities, to more effectively document decision paths, and to understand how costs are incurred and behave.
The next few sections will define degrees of freedom and will discuss
how they are used in an ECD environment. These sections will

1. focus on defining what a degree of freedom is in the context
   of management decisions.

2. discuss how managers can create and destroy degrees of freedom. This concept will be important when considering project and program management.

3. discuss how to create dependencies among decisions (a concept referred to as *coupling*). This section will also discuss how to identify decoupling and how to decouple decisions and actions.

WHAT IS A DEGREE OF FREEDOM?

Degree of freedom is a term often used in certain engineering disciplines that represents an entity's physical options of motion. When applied properly in this case, degrees of freedom involve translation and rotation. For example, the translation, or linear movement, of a tire involves more than just going forward. It has the ability to move forward because nothing constrains it from doing so, and it also has the freedom to rotate because nothing constrains it from rotating. So, a tire translates along one axis and rotates around another axis. To simplify the discussion, only translation will be used as a metaphor for introducing degrees of freedom for management purposes.

An object that can move only forward and backward in one plane has one degree of freedom; that is, the object can move only in one dimension. Train tracks limit the movement of a train to essentially one plane (Exhibit 6.1), for the train cannot move perpendicular to the direction of this plane. The plane in which the train travels may change, suggesting that a train does not always have to go north and south, for instance. As a train track curves, a train momentarily may be headed in a northeasterly direction. Although the tracks may curve, the train is still limited to the direction parallel to the track. At this point, the train can go either northeast or south-

Exhibit 6.1   A Train Is Limited to Forward and Backward Motion Only

west. It does not have the freedom to go in a direction that is perpendicular to the tracks.

A person walking, however, has the freedom to move in a two-dimensional space (Exhibit 6.2). The person can choose to go forward, backward, left, or right and is not limited to just going forward of backward as the train is. The design of the train and how it interacts with the tracks purposely limits the movement options, or the degrees of freedom, of a train. Since a person walking is not limited to tracks, that person has the freedom to move freely in a two-dimensional plane (in the absence of constraints such as walls, of course) and can choose to walk forward, to walk diagonally, or to step to the side with all the same relative ease.

A helicopter has the ability to move in all three planes (Exhibit 6.3). In addition to the two planes described previously, which allow the helicopter to go forward, backward, left or right, the helicopter can also go up and down in a vertical plane. As a result of having three degrees of freedom, the helicopter pilot has more decision options. To get to the other side of a mountain, for instance, the pilot can choose to simply go around the mountain or to go over it. Since they are limited to two degrees of freedom, people must take whatever paths the road allows them to take.

Through effective design, it is possible to increase or decrease the number of degrees of freedom that an object will have. For example, the structure for a bridge allows for movement in the

Exhibit 6.2   A Person Walking Has the Option to Move in Any Direction of 360 Degrees in a Two-Dimensional Plane

Exhibit 6.3   The Helicopter Has Complete Freedom to Move in
Any Direction in Three-Dimensional Space.

direction along the length of the bridge, because the bridge will expand and contract with changes in the weather. The structure must be able to handle this movement, so engineers design the structure to allow the movement to happen. If a bridge were able to move in directions perpendicular to its length, it would be possible for the bridge to fall down or be knocked over on its side. In design, engineers use techniques that basically will eliminate degrees of freedom. By doing so, the bridge moves in directions that are desirable and does not move in the directions that are not. Similarly, a helicopter is designed to have more degrees of freedom than a train has.

More degrees of freedom bring more complexity. The movement of the helicopter offers many more options for the pilot than the movement options of the train does for the train engineer. Life is relatively simple when the choices are basically go forward or go backward. Since the choices of whether to go up or to the right are not available, directional issues are relatively less complicated.

Although not exactly the same, management decision making is fairly similar to physical motion. A manager might face a number of decision-making options, or degrees of freedom, when addressing a particular situation. For example, a manager can choose to act or to not act—two degrees of freedom—in a situation. Selecting one degree of freedom and the resulting implementation eliminates the second degree of freedom for this decision but might open other degrees of freedom in the situation that results from the implementation.

Consider a manager who is faced with capacity constraints. The manager may have three degrees of freedom. First, the manager can choose to not work at full production, in which case the manager is limiting the availability of items for the organization to sell. Assume that the manager selected this option. Although there is demand for the product, the manager chooses to work the employees at 95 percent. From an ECD perspective, the resource costs are still the same, so the organization is paying for 40 hours of work but is receiving only 38 hours of work. In this situation, the decision has been made, and the manager must live with the consequences—whether positive or negative. What are the consequences? Someone in the organization should be looking at why production is not meeting demand. If this person finds that the manager is not getting all from the employees that could be realized, dissatisfaction is likely to occur. The manager likely has reasons for the decision, including that the manager could achieve the performance numbers expected from the department without working the people at 100 percent. If this were the case, the organization might want to revisit the performance measures that may have been established in times of lower demand or may not have considered the organizational impact of the constraint operation. After determining the new metrics, the manager might choose from one of the other degrees of freedom.

Second, the manager can choose to have production work at full capacity so that the operations are potentially maximized. In this scenario, the manager decides to work the employees at 100 percent and may be encouraged to not incur overtime. By not incurring overtime, the manager seeks to maximize the possible output given the desire of management to not increase labor costs. Although this scenario might be more desirable than working the employees 95 percent of the time, it still keeps the organization from achieving maximum revenues.

Third, the manager can choose to have production work overtime to meet the demand for the products. If management had determined that the incremental cost increase was more than compensated by the revenue achieved by meeting the market demand, it might make sense to work overtime. The initial concerns would be based on the analysis. To incur overtime suggests that resource costs will temporarily increase, leading to an increased resource cost recovery requirement. However, the amount of the overtime should be determinable, and if the demand is there, it is likely that the revenues received from incurring the overtime will at least offset the costs.

This summarizes the three degrees of freedom available to this manager. Notice that cost savings is really not addressed here. In a capacity-constrained environment, the focus of managing operations should be on maintaining reasonable costs. The difficulty for most managers in a time of high growth or high demand is managing costs. The temptation from a cost management perspective might be to either grow along with the markets, or to constrain growth, which might keep the organization from reaching its financial optimum.

What will happen if capacity doubles and the organization is no longer capacity constrained? The excess capacity creates additional degrees of freedom. The original three degrees of freedom still exist: the organization can scale back operations to some level below 100 percent, it can continue to operate at 100 percent, or it can choose to work overtime. The last two degrees of freedom may not make sense. Why make employees work overtime when there is no demand for the product? While such a practice might make sense in a highly seasonal market, hopefully planning would be such that overtime would be avoided. The organization also can choose to operate at 100 percent; this decision might be questionable from a cost management perspective, however, because costs are not being reduced by operating at a higher than necessary rate.

If the organization has excess capacity, it may choose to operate at some level below 100 percent. Being able to meet demand while operating below 100 percent suggests a condition of overcapacity. Clearly, when the organization can complete all of the scheduled work and still have time to spare, there is either not enough work or too much time. The result is that the capacity exceeds the demand placed on it. This condition might create additional degrees of freedom. Although reducing capacity was an option when operating at less than 100 percent of capacity, it was not necessarily a viable option. In an overcapacity condition, however, reducing capacity might now be an option. *Might* is the operative word because creating a degree of freedom will *require* that enough excess capacity is created so that resources can be cut. An organization cannot reduce its capacity by one worker with a 5 percent saving in time. By creating enough capacity that one worker is no longer needed, an additional degree of freedom is created.

Programs themselves often do not reduce costs. As discussed previously, the program that doubled available capacity did not reduce the costs. With the excess resources, the organization can still choose not to cut the costs. Programs may increase the degrees of freedom that decision makers have, which often can allow the manager to select a degree that will allow for cost cutting if that is the result being sought. With additional capacity, resource costs can now be cut, or they can be kept. The viable choice exists for the manager.

CREATING AND DESTROYING DEGREES OF FREEDOM

Suggestions for operational change and operational improvement often center on creating degrees of freedom, which, if chosen, can improve operations. Productivity enhancements are often improvements of this type. Since a degree of freedom is a choice, enhancements can be created by adding to the existing choices available to an organization. Although universally applicable, this discussion will focus on creating and destroying profit-oriented degrees of freedom.

Creating degrees of freedom simply involves increasing the available choices in a situation. Think of driving along the freeway. By driving in the center of three lanes on the freeway, the driver essentially has three degrees of freedom. If an event were to occur that required evasive measures, the driver could either go forward, go to the left lane, or go to the right lane. Destroying degrees of freedom involves eliminating, sometimes temporarily, available choices. In the freeway example, driving in either the far left lane or the far right lane eliminates one degree of freedom. The driver in the left lane can now either go straight or go to the center lane (unless going off of the freeway is considered an option). By choosing to drive in the center lane rather than the right lane, the driver now has increased her options by one degree of freedom.

It is possible to select one option from a set of options, and this selection can increase the number of subsequent options. Through this selection, the number of degrees of freedom has increased. This can especially be the case when managing programs to manage costs. Each decision may either create cost degrees of freedom or destroy cost degrees of freedom. Because their dynamics are different, creating and destroying cost degrees of freedom might require different techniques. Therefore, since there are three types of costs, each one will be addressed individually.

Creating and Destroying Resource Cost Degrees of Freedom

Since resource costs are generally capacity related or operationally focused, degrees of freedom are typically created by increasing organizational capacity without increasing the resource costs. Efficiency-oriented tasks often have the ability to increase organizational capacity. By increasing efficiency, organizations may find that it takes fewer resources to get the same work done, thus creating the potential for additional degrees of freedom. Overall process improvement might have an impact as well. By redesigning or completely reengineering a process, the idea is to improve the process such that fewer resources are required to get the job done. The net effect is an increase in capacity. The other way to increase resource cost degrees of freedom is to look for ways to change the cost of the resource. If an option surfaces for cheaper resources, such as going offshore for programming help, an additional degree of freedom becomes available.

When at or above capacity, managers often need all of their resources and sometimes more. They do not have the option to cut resources unless there are extenuating circumstances that are beyond the immediate optimization of the organization's finances. To aid in cutting costs from a capacity perspective, anything that can be done to increase capacity without significantly increasing resource costs might create additional degrees of freedom. For managers, these additional degrees of freedom create options that help them make decisions to reduce costs.

One example of increasing degrees of freedom for cost cutting is automating an operation in a manufacturing environment. Assume that a worker who makes widget components has responsibilities that can be automated by a robot. Unless the worker's responsibilities cease as soon as the robot goes online, there will be extra capacity. With the extra capacity comes more degrees of freedom. Previously, options with this worker may not have existed. With automating the process, the organization might choose to put the worker in a higher, value-added position, which does not cut costs, or it might choose to lay off the worker, which will cut costs.

Destroying resource cost degrees of freedom is not bad. In this case, *to destroy* means to take away a viable option. One way that this can be done is to take away an option by mandate. For example, an organization with a no-layoff policy destroys the degree of freedom that is centered on reducing the workforce. Another example would be to align capacity with demand. For example, in the case described earlier when capacity was doubled, by adjusting the resources so that they are aligned with the demand, there is no longer a degree of freedom available associated with reducing resource costs. The action itself reduced the cost.

Creating and Destroying Action Cost Degrees of Freedom

To create an action cost degree of freedom, the goal is to create options that either would reduce the number of times that an action must occur or would reduce the cost of each action. An example of reducing the number of times an action must occur would be to focus on optimizing shipping, which is an action cost. The more an organization ships, the more it costs. By figuring out how to reduce the number of LTL (less than truckload) shipments, the organization now has the option to ship fewer times. Managers can choose to use the new information and reduce the number of shipments. They also can choose to continue to ship as they have in the past, which will, of course, keep the costs the same. Managers can also create degrees of freedom by finding alternatives that can reduce the cost of an action. For example, there might be an organization that can reduce overall shipping costs for each load. The option to go with the new lower priced shipping company creates another degree of freedom for the organization. The organization can choose to look into both options in this case. For example, the organization might solicit the help of a consulting company that can help with the overall optimization of the logistics operations. This might include optimizing truckloads and routing options, which may lead to truckload savings and additional degrees of freedom associated with both the cost for each truckload and the number of truckloads.

Another option is to destroy degrees of freedom by acting to eliminate options that exist. By going with a lower priced trucking service vendor, an organization might eliminate the option to go with the higher priced vendor. This has eliminated the need to consider the higher priced vendor altogether.

Creating and Destroying Item Cost Degrees of Freedom

Creating item cost degrees of freedom involves, as with action costs, either reducing the number of items to be purchased or reducing the cost of each item. Quality improvements are examples of how to reduce the number of items being purchased. It is well documented that manufacturing organizations must plan to buy more materials because of expected defects, damage, and setup requirements that will consume materials. Therefore, to make 100 parts, the organization might have to purchase 110 components (expecting that 10 will be lost to processing). Increasing the quality of the processes may drive this number down toward 100, therefore reducing the need to buy 110 components. The organization may still choose to buy 110 items, suggesting that the quality improvement itself does not save the cost. Instead, the actions resulting from the improvement can lead to the cost savings.

Strategic sourcing and electronic procurement, or e-procurment, software may provide the opportunity to create item cost degrees of freedom. Ideally, with strategic sourcing, relationships are established with vendors that should ultimately help the vendor reduce its cost of operation and pass some of the savings on to the customer. Only when savings are passed on to the organization will strategic sourcing have a bottom-line impact. The vendor may choose not to pass on the savings, just as the organization may choose not to purchase from the strategic partner. However, the degrees of freedom do allow for the cost-reduction-oriented choices.

E-procurement software is an example of how to reduce degrees of freedom. With an effective e-procurement implementation and supporting procurement rules, those purchasing items using the technology will be assured that the price they are paying for an item is the lowest possible price that the organization has contracted. For example, if the organization has a contract to buy pencils at $5.00 per box, by using the e-procurement software, the buyer will not pay the $5.80 to a competitor with whom there is no contract. The software eliminates degrees of freedom itself by adhering to business rules implemented in the software.

COUPLED AND DECOUPLED DECISIONS AND PROGRAM JUSTIFICATION

As is apparent from the creating and destroying degrees of freedom discussion, having an option available does not necessarily mean that it will be chosen and that the organization will be improved. The fact that an option exists allows for those with decision-making responsibility to choose an action that is not necessarily the best for the organization overall. Of course, managers usually do not intentionally do things that are bad for the organization. However, given the measurement systems and management styles that are often in place, lower level managers may not have the proper visibility of the organization to understand the real impact of their decisions.

When improvements are made or suggested, they often create multiple degrees of freedom. Even if millions of dollars in savings opportunities from quality improvements are identified, the organization still can choose to not take advantage of the identified savings. At this point, the decisions are decoupled; that is, they do not exist together as one decision/implementation pair. Savings and operational improvements will occur when the decision-making points are coupled into an implementable pair with results that have an identifiable bottom-line impact. The usual tendency of an organization is to remain at status quo. As shown in Exhibit 6.4, although the organization is not coupled, if nothing is done, it will not improve. Often, organizations do not always do what they think or know is right

Exhibit 6.4 Organizations Often Have Barriers That Keep Change from Occurring

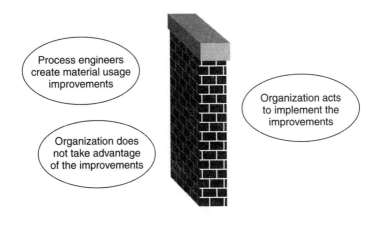

Exhibit 6.5   By Going Over the Wall and Forcing Coupling to
Occur, Improvements Will Take Place and Will Smash
the Status Quo

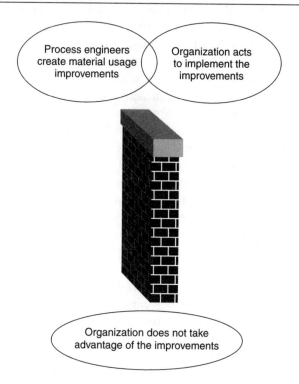

even when the improvement is well known and accepted.[1] Only
when the organization goes over the decision-making wall and forces
the decisions to be coupled will there be improvement (Exhibit 6.5).

When justifying programs, it is important to take the next step
and identify the coupling necessary to improve the organization. To
help this occur, when looking at the economics of a program, the following three components should be in place:

1. Identify the path to profit enhancement whether through cost
   reductions, revenue enhancements, or both.
2. Identify the decision-making points that are necessary to reach
   the cost-reduction path.
3. Identify, in detail, how the improvement will increase the degrees of freedom necessary to achieve the desired improvement.

It is important to understand that improvements often do not just happen. When justifying programs and making decisions, foremost in the mind of the decision maker from a cost perspective is: "What is the bottom-line impact of what I am proposing?" From there, the focus should be on obtaining the bottom-line impact by using the improvement opportunity to create degrees of freedom that others can use to drive improvements throughout the organization. This focus and dedication will help ensure that improvements are made in the organization.

Endnote

[1]Jeffrey Pfeffer, *The Knowing-Doing Gap: How Smart Companies Turn Knowledge into Action* (Boston: Harvard Business School Press, 2000).

7

Operational Inconsistencies

Over time, certain rules and techniques become so ingrained in our thinking that they are taken for granted. One example of this is the idea of costs decreasing as a worker does more. This is physically and mathematically impossible. Certain techniques incorrectly suggest that when time is saved, costs automatically decrease, leading to more profitable operating conditions. From our discussions of explicit cost dynamics (ECD) and degree of freedom management, it should be clear that saving time does not always equate to cost savings. The result of time savings is often more degrees of freedom available to a manager so that costs subsequently can be reduced. Because these concepts are so widely used and because they often violate the law of conservation of dollars and the fundamentals of ECD, it makes sense to discuss each in detail to help clarify which concepts can or do make sense. The concepts discussed in this chapter are learning and experience curves, economies of scale, optimum order quantities, and machine utilization and efficiency.

LEARNING AND EXPERIENCE CURVE

When an increased cumulative volume of a product or service is created or performed with the same resources, it is assumed that efficiency of creating or performing increases. This phenomenon has been observed in many industries and is often measured and reported as the *rate of improvement*. The simple assumption is that the more a person does something, the better that person becomes at it. This has been shown in many psychological and physical studies over time. We all have experienced this phenomenon when learning how to ride a bicycle, for example, or when doing our jobs every day. We find more efficient and effective ways to perform tasks. At first, this improvement rate might appear to be fairly rapid—50 percent, 60 percent, and even more. Realistically, over time, the opportunities for improving a specific process may slow down and only slight improvements if any are made.

Many studies have been performed with the objective of quantifying the rate of learning. In general, the rate of improvement can be expressed graphically or mathematically by the learning curve equation (Equation 7.1). It is commonly proposed that, theoretically, direct labor hours are reduced by a relatively constant percentage with every doubling in total volume.[1] This proposal is represented by the expression found in Equation 7.1. T_i represents the time that it should take to produce the ith unit. So, in estimating the time that it would take to produce the 100th unit, T_i would be 100. T_1 represents the amount of time that it took to make the first unit. In this equation, i would just be the unit number for which the analysis is trying to determine the production time.

$$T_i = T_1 i^r \qquad (7.1)$$

In this equation, the variable r represents the slope of the learning curve,[2] which can be determined by creating a logarithmic ratio involving the rate of learning, n, and a constant value of 2 (Equation 7.2). Thus, if an organization has a learning rate of 85 percent, n would be 85 percent. In this equation, n represents the rate of improvement for each doubling in total quantity.

$$r = \frac{\ln n}{\ln 2} \qquad (7.2)$$

To help understand how this works, consider the following example: An organization that makes a product finds that when it doubles the total quantity being made, the production time is about 70 percent of the original time. Thus, its learning rate is 70 percent. If the first unit took 2 hours to produce, how long will it take to produce the 10th item?

First, by applying Equation 7.2, the slope of the learning curve must be determined.

$$r = \frac{\ln 0.7}{\ln 2}$$
$$= \frac{-0.3567}{0.6931}$$
$$= -0.5146$$

To determine the length of time to produce the 10th item, Equation 7.1 is used. In this case, T_1 is 2 hours and i is 10. Therefore,

$$T_i = 2 \times 10^{-0.5146}$$
$$= 0.6115 \text{ Hours}$$
$$\approx 36 \text{ Minutes}$$

With learning rate information, it is possible to predict how many labor hours might be needed for any particular item. The next logical step would be to try to tie this improvement to the cost of a unit as efficiency increases. If the second unit takes 70 percent of the time the first unit takes and the fourth unit takes 70 percent of the second, the fourth must be less costly than the second and the second less costly than the first. According to Hayes and Wheelwright, "The experience curve is simply an extension of the manufacturing progress function/learning curve, where the relationship of interest is that between the cost (rather than the labor hours) per unit and cumulative volume ('experience')."[3]

To accomplish this, labor hours are determined from learning curve calculations and are used in a cost equation. For example, using traditional measures, total cost is expressed as shown in Equation 7.3.

$$TC = F_c + V_c \qquad (7.3)$$

Total variable cost is determined by taking the product of the unit variable cost and the number of units produced. If V_{cu} is the variable cost per unit and U is the number of units produced, Equation 7.4 describes the total cost function in this simple world.

$$TC = F_c + \Sigma[V_{cu} \times U] \qquad (7.4)$$

For direct labor allocation, the variable cost consists of a material portion, a direct labor portion, and a burden portion. The direct labor portion and the burden portion often are assumed to vary with changes in direct labor hours. Through a little calculus (integrating Equation 7.1 with respect to i and dividing by the total number of units produced), an average time per unit can be calculated (Equation 7.5). Simply, if the time for each unit (although changing) is known, by adding the total time for each unit, a cumulative time can be determined for all items through the ith. By dividing by i (the total number of units), an average time per unit is derived.

$$T_{av} = \frac{T_{total}}{i} = T_1 \frac{i_r}{r + 1} \qquad (7.5)$$

From this development, ultimately it can be assumed that the unit cost of production will go down as the number of units increases. If M is the material cost for each unit, D_r is the direct labor cost for each unit, B_r is the burden rate, and T_{av} is the average time per unit, then as T_{av} goes down, the cost per unit goes down (Equation 7.6)

$$V_{cu} \approx M + D_r \times (1 + B_r) \times T_{av}$$
$$\approx M + D_r \times (1 + B_r) \times T_1 \frac{i_r}{r + 1} \qquad (7.6)$$

The problem with the development of Equation 7.6 is the assumption that costs change with changes in direct labor hours. What is incorrect about the experience curve concept is that costs do not automatically go down as direct labor hours decrease (see Chapter 6). While it may take less time to perform an action, unless there is less money leaving the organization, costs have not decreased. It is not a general rule that production workers are paid less for being more productive. Overhead does not go down with efficiency, and there is usually no bottom-line impact to be achieved from experience. Although the fact that degrees of freedom can increase with experience is a good thing, in and of itself, experience does not reduce costs.

Assume, for example, that a production worker becomes twice as fast and can now complete eight hours worth of work in four. The worker now can spend the rest of the time completing additional work, performing preventive maintenance, or doing some combination of the two. In this case, fewer dollars do not leave the organization. Since total cost, the cost measure that helps determine profitability, is a monotonically increasing function, costs do not go down as efficiency increases. Cost reductions in the form of fewer repair costs from breakdowns, which are avoided by preventive maintenance, are the result of a management action to spend time performing this activity. The free time itself does not lead to this cost avoidance—management action does.

Although mathematically rigorous, such developments can lead to situations that do not necessarily lead to more profitable operating conditions as a result of lowering costs.

ECONOMIES OF SCALE

The concept of economies of scale is based on the idea that total manufacturing costs rise more slowly than production volume.[4]

However, this is only one of many aspects of economies of scale. According to Hayes and Wheelwright, there are three types of economies of scale that are based on different aspects of total cost: (1) short-term, (2) intermediate-term, and (3) long-term economies.

Short-Term Economies

Short-term economies of scale focus on reducing the unit cost of a product. When dividing fixed costs by the total number of units produced, as the number of units increases, the cost per unit decreases.[5] This type of economy of scale is referred to as *short term* because fixed costs are, in fact, assumed fixed only during short periods of time. As the fixed costs change, the concept must be reapplied to address the specifics of the new scenario.

Intermediate-Term Economies

The intermediate-term economy of scale deals with cost reduction by lowering what are referred to here as action costs. Wheelwright and Hayes focus on the reduction in frequency of activities so that the cost of the activity per unit goes down. Their concepts suggest that by increasing the number of units between activities, for example, the activity cost per unit is decreased. By dedicating resources, they argue, other costs can be reduced as well. Fewer changeovers, lesser skilled workers, and shorter processing time can result from either assigning or designing equipment that will be used specifically for resources to a given product, line, or family.

Long-Term Economies of Scale

Hayes and Wheelwright divide long-term economies of scale into static economies of scale and dynamic economies of scale.

Static Economies of Scale

Static economies of scale, they suggest, exist as a result of being able to use one large machine rather than numerous small machines to perform a task or multiple tasks. Their argument is that production volume is related to the volume of a machine and cost is related to its surface area. Since volume increases faster than surface area when purchasing a machine, production volume will increase faster than costs.[6]

Dynamic Economies of Scale

Dynamic economies of scale result from increases of efficiencies at a particular level that lead to improvements in production rates. For example, on a given machine, as more parts are produced, it is expected that the time per unit will decrease.

Analyzing the Economies of Scale

The basis for economies of scale is the unit cost. In every case, it is assumed that the unit cost decreases as economies of scale are realized. With short-term economies of scale, the focus is on trying to get the most out of a cost while it is in its fixed range; the more this is accomplished, the cheaper it must be. With intermediate-term economies of scale, the rule is basically the same, for the emphasis essentially is on reducing the action cost per unit. With longer term economies, the fundamental goal is to get the most from resource costs. Buying larger machines and increasing the rates at which they are run should lead to longer-term economies of scale.

Although there are benefits to be had from these concepts, which Hayes and Wheelwright suggest come from a reduction in the cost per unit, the *savings* do not come from a reduction in the cost of a unit of production. True enough, cost reductions will often occur with intermediate-term economies if a worker is performing an activity less frequently. However, most of the other financial improvements are from an increase in output given the same or similar input. Consider the following example. Assume that over a fixed period, the resource costs are \$100.00. Additionally, assume that one activity is performed at a cost of \$35.00. Finally, the item cost per unit is \$10.00. The expression for total costs is found using Equation 7.7 (which also appeared as Equation 5.2).

$$\text{Total Cost} = \Sigma \, \text{Resource Costs} + \Sigma \, \text{Action Costs} + \Sigma \, \text{Item Costs} \quad (7.7)$$

Dividing by the number of units produced leads to the cost per unit relationship shown in Equation 7.7.

$$\frac{\text{Total Cost}}{\text{Units Produced}} = \frac{\Sigma \, \text{Resource Costs}}{\text{Units Produced}} + \frac{\Sigma \, \text{Action Costs}}{\text{Units Produced}} + \frac{\Sigma \, \text{Item Costs}}{\text{Units Produced}} \quad (7.8)$$

Assume, further, that there is a one-to-one correlation between the number of units produced and the number of items purchased. In other words, one item goes into each unit produced. In this case, the item cost per unit is simply the cost of the item. Simplifying Equation 7.8 leads to Equation 7.9.

$$\frac{\text{Total Cost}}{\text{Units Produced}} = \frac{\Sigma\,(\text{Resource Cost} + \text{Action Costs})}{\text{Units Produced}} + \text{Item Cost} \quad (7.9)$$

From this relationship, it can be assumed that as the number of units produced increases, the total cost per unit goes down. Applying the data from the example, Equation 7.9 becomes the cost per unit equation (Equation 7.10). To develop an expression for total costs, simply multiply by the number of units being produced. The result is Equation 7.11.

$$\frac{TC}{\text{Units Produced}} = \frac{\$135.00}{\text{Units Produced}} + \frac{\$10.00 \times \text{Units Produced}}{\text{Units Produced}} \quad (7.10)$$

$$= \frac{\$135.00}{\text{Units Produced}} + \$10.00$$

$$TC = \$135.00 + \$10.00 \times \text{Units Produced} \quad (7.11)$$

Applying Equation 7.10, to produce 10 units, the total cost per unit would be $23.50 (Equation 7.12).

$$\frac{TC}{U} = \frac{\$135.00}{10} + \$10.00 = \$23.50 \quad (7.12)$$

To produce 100 units, the total cost per unit would be $11.35 (Equation 7.13).

$$\frac{TC}{U} = \frac{\$135.00}{100} + \$10.00 = \$11.35 \quad (7.13)$$

The data suggest that making more units will achieve economies of scale and will reduce the cost of doing business. However, consider what happens when factoring in total cost so that profitability can be determined.

To produce 10 units, the total cost would be $235.00, as shown in Equation 7.14. Now, assume that with the same resources and the same actions (long and intermediate economies), 100 units are produced. Clearly, the item costs will increase. The resulting total cost is $1,135.00, as found in Equation 7.15.

$$TC = \$100.00 + \$35.00 + \$10.00 \times 10 = \$235.00 \quad (7.14)$$

$$TC = \$100.00 + \$35.00 + \$10.00 \times 100 = \$1,135.00 \quad (7.15)$$

Although it is more costly to produce 100 units than it is to produce 10, the unit cost goes down. Only if there is demand for the product will an organization make money from selling more products. What is the difference? Should the organization make 1,000 units if there is no demand for them? No, they should not even if the cost is much lower. The cost per unit does not matter. What matters is that there is demand for the product. In the example just discussed, if the organization made 100 units and had demand for only 50, its position would not be too good.

Assume that demand exists and that each unit sells for $30.00. The profit for this transaction is determined by the difference between revenues and costs, which is $65.00 (Equation 7.16). As determined by Equation 7.17, if there were demand for 100 units, the profit is $1,865.00.

$$\text{Profit} = \$30.00 \times 10 - \$235.00 = \$65.00 \qquad (7.16)$$

$$\text{Profit} = \$30.00 \times 100 - \$1{,}135.00 = \$1{,}865.00 \qquad (7.17)$$

In the second scenario, the organization is actually more profitable. The improvement is simply the result of getting more revenues from the organization's resources over a period of time rather than lowering the cost per unit by increasing volumes.

With resource costs and action costs exactly the same and item costs increasing, the revenue generation must be the difference. Revenues are increasing at a faster rate than the costs being subtracted from it. The revenue line increases at a rate equal to the price ($30.00 per unit in this case), while the cost line (constant activity and resource costs reduce costs to a line rather than a surface) increases at a rate equal to the item cost ($10.00 per unit in this case). Clearly, the difference between the two lines is greater when producing more units. Now, the important question: If you were the manager, would you take a selling price of $20.00? Why or why not? The answer to a similar question will be discussed in the Chapter 9 case study section.

Benefits from Economies of Scale

Three benefits can be gained from economies of scale. The first benefit comes from the increased degrees of freedom associated with time savings, which result from minimizing activities necessary to perform a job. The second is the potential for an increased cost recovery ratio (CRR) as a result of getting more revenue from an organization's resources over a fixed period of time. In actuality, one can lead to the other if the right conditions exist—namely, demand for product and proper management. The third is increased knowledge gained from *dynamic economies of scale*, as defined previously. New and innovative ways to operate should be the norm for most organizations.

OPTIMUM ORDER QUANTITIES

One of the most interesting models to analyze from an ECD perspective is the optimum order quantity (OOQ) model. The basis for this model is the belief that when performing an activity such as ordering materials, some costs go up as more materials are ordered and some costs go down as more materials are ordered. This statement should automatically generate skepticism, for to develop these models, it is first suggested that the average cost over a period is determined using the item cost, order cost, carrying cost, and shortage cost.[7] The order cost and some shortage costs are assumed to decrease as more units are purchased, while item costs, carrying costs, and other shortage costs are assumed to increase as more units are purchased. The goal is to mathematically find a balance between the two, and the resulting value is the OOQ. As we have seen previously, however, cost functions are monotonically increasing functions. It is easy to see, therefore, that if all costs increase, the OOQ to minimize costs would be to not order! Since companies must order, however, the emphasis should not be placed on minimizing costs—it should be on maximizing profits. Unfortunately, OOQ models typically emphasize cost minimization rather than profit maximization.

Item Costs

If an item is purchased from another entity, there is really no ambiguity regarding the cost to the organization. The transaction cost is visible to anyone wanting and needing to see it. However, what if the item comes from another division within the same organization? How does one handle non-purchased goods? One definition of non-purchased item costs is the unit variable cost of production,[8] which is where questions regarding the assumptions begin to surface. If the unit variable cost has any allocations associated with it, one of the fundamental costs used in the development is flawed from the beginning. If a program and a unit were one and the same, as is the case when ordering an airplane, the truly variable cost could be determined. For a single screw in a batch of screws being produced, it cannot. The materials were likely purchased for the program, and the labor is constant. Only the utilities could be defined for that single screw.

Setup and Order Costs

If there is a cost to set up machines or to order products, this cost is independent of the number of units produced.[9] Since they only exist if the action is performed, they are action costs. The following two issues must be considered:

1. What parts of these actions are true costs (money leaving the organization)?
2. Are these costs being allocated?

True Costs

What is the true cost to set up a machine? If a machine is set up by an hourly production worker, maintenance worker, or job setter, there is no additional cost for labor. Only when someone from outside is hired to set up a machine will the labor costs associated with setting up the machine change. However, this is exactly contrary to traditional management thinking which suggests: "When a machine is prepared for a production run to resupply an inventory of finished goods, the fixed setup cost may include the labor and overhead required to prepare the machine and the opportunity cost of the time the machine is not used productively."[10]

To suggest that there is a cost associated with someone already on the payrolls performing a task associated with the worker's regular pay violates the law of conservation of dollars. The hourly pay is a cost of doing business whether the worker is setting up machines, running parts, or doing nothing at all. Additionally, to suggest that there is a cost associated with machine downtime is equally wrong. If the machine is a constraint to meeting market demand, the organization loses revenues. If the machine is not a constraint, nothing is lost.[11] Therefore, costs that are not even true costs are being allocated to setting up a machine.

Regarding ordering costs, Mathur & Solow mention that "When placing an order, the cost . . . may include the clerical and management times needed to prepare the order, a charge for transmitting the order by fax, for example, and a fixed charge by the supplier for processing and/or delivering the order."[12]

Again, this is misleading. There is no additional cost for a clerical worker to fill out an order. If there is an overtime charge for this action, it is because the worker has been given work that exceeds the worker's capacity or the order was given at the wrong time with a high priority. Either the worker is efficient but has been given too much, or the worker is inefficient and needs more time to get things done. In either case, these costs have nothing to do with the order. They are general or cost management issues that should be left out of the cost of a product. The only cost associated with the example of faxing an order is the cost of the long-distance phone call. The machine toner, and paper are sunk costs.

The only true cost in this example is the cost charged by the customer for filling the order. The effect of this cost on the bottom line is the same for each time the activity occurs. Clearly, it might be possible to manage total cost by ordering fewer times. This is not, however, a cost per unit issue; rather, it is a cost management issue.

Shortage or Stockout Costs

Shortages or stockouts are assumed to occur when there is demand for product that is not available. Varied costs—for example, shutdown and idle-time costs,[13] backorder costs,[14] discount-type costs, and goodwill costs[15]—are assumed to exist from such a situation.

Shutdown costs might occur if scrap is produced while bringing the production system up to or down from a steady-state operating level. Other than that, costs should be the same. Action costs associated with ordering cost might exist, as more expediting might be necessary. Air freight, for example, might be more expensive than sending the same package by ground. This is an action cost that is more a function of the order than of the unit. Discount costs might be incurred by an organization either from trying to maintain satisfied customers by penalizing itself (such as providing a 5 percent discount) or through some sort of external penalty (such as allowing a customer to pay so much less per item for each week late).[16] Finally, there is the cost of goodwill. Late orders might prevent a customer from ordering again from the organization, just as not having something in stock at a walk-in facility might deter a customer from buying at that store.

The only true costs are the action costs associated with expediting orders. Goodwill, penalties, and filling out additional ordering paperwork do not cost more money. They do, however, reduce the degrees of freedom that exist for gaining profit. For example, the lost revenues from goodwill might be difficult to regain. Time and effort might be spent building the organization's reputation or marketing to a larger pool of potential customers rather than in maintaining an already good reputation or existing customers. Likewise, penalties reduce revenues; they do not increase costs. Instead of getting $50.00, the organization now gets $40.00. Again, the total cost does not change; the revenues do.

Carrying or Holding Costs

The concept of carrying cost is straightforward. A certain amount is charged for storing a product or for tying up the money used to purchase the items. For instance, warehouse costs might be allocated to the cost of a product, which is an example of allocating a resource cost to the product level. When rented, warehouses typically are rented either as a whole or in part. Nevertheless, the costs generally are based on space and not on the number of items in inventory. Payment based on the number of items in inventory would be similar to charging rent for an apartment based on the number of pieces of furniture the tenant has. Instead, warehouse costs (that is, rent payments) generally are fixed over a given period.

If there were an insurance cost per unit, it might be associated with the individual product level. For nonimportant inventory items, however, it is more likely to be tied to the program, set of programs, or superprograms that led to the batch of inventory than to a single item. For example, while a car dealer may have to insure every single BMW, the screw manufacturer will not have to insure every screw.

With OOQ models, there are too many inconsistencies to take them seriously. The fundamental assumption about costs decreasing is wrong. In each case where there is an assumed cost involved, the costs are often not true costs and the models often assume some sort of allocation of even the artificially created costs. Most importantly, the models do not include profit as a decision variable. For these reasons, it is not difficult to understand why the late Shigeo Shingo, one of the fathers of just in time (JIT), said economic lots, are "an evasive measure and in no way a positive approach to production."[17] In fact, according to Shingo, the concept *economic lot sizes* is no longer taught in Japanese profitability accounting courses.

MACHINE UTILIZATION AND EFFICIENCY

A common belief in manufacturing environments is that machines must be utilized because, somehow, this pays off the machine. Paying for an expensive machine that sits idle is a waste of money, say the traditionalists. Use the machine so that it can pay for itself. The question is: Does using a machine more make it pay for itself faster? Not necessarily. Does using the machine more often and more frequently reduce costs? No. Machine utilization and efficiency are measures often used to ensure that the most is achieved from people and processes. Utilization, U, compares the amount of time a resource was utilized to how much it was available to be utilized (Equation 7.18)

$$U = \frac{\text{Time Utilized}}{\text{Time Available}} \qquad (7.18)$$

Efficiency, E, compares the amount of time a resource was actually utilized to how long a machine was able to be utilized (Equation 7.19). Efficiency can take on many forms, such as an expected standard time (input) versus actual time (output) or expected number of parts produced (input) versus actual parts produced (output).

$$E = \frac{\text{Output}}{\text{Input}} \qquad (7.19)$$

Although noble in their efforts, when used by themselves, these measures can be dangerous. Ultimately, the objective of these measures is to reduce costs. Utilization is a ratio that suggests that an organization always wants to use a resource and wants to get the most out of that resource. However, that might not be a desirable situation to promote. Additionally, the measures could lead to poorer operating conditions for the organization. Consider the production system represented in Exhibit 7.1. In this case, operation 1 takes raw materials, processes them, then passes them on to operation 2. Operation 2 processes them and creates finished goods. Clearly, the maximum throughput of the process is five units per hour. Running the first operation at any rate greater than the rate necessary to sustain the second operation is wasted effort.[18]

Exhibit 7.1   Example of a Two-Step Production System

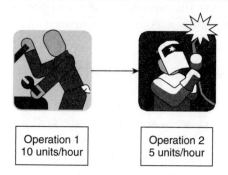

Operation 1 10 units/hour	Operation 2 5 units/hour

However, in an environment where utilization and efficiency are measured, different behavior might be observed. Where utilization is important, the organization must try to use the resource for the entire time that it is available. When considered without efficiency, the organization can keep the utilization up by reducing the throughput. Using Exhibit 7.1 as a reference, the operation could conceivably operate at 50 percent of its maximum capability and achieve 100 percent utilization while feeding the second operation. The problem is, if the standard rate is 10 units per hour, the incentive might be to operate the first operation at 10 units per hour rather than the process-governed 5 units per hour. If this is the case, the organization might run the first operation at maximum utilization and efficiency *to keep the cost of that operation down*. What happens, however, is that the cost of the overall operations increases. Operation 1 consumes materials at twice the rate that operation 2 can, which will lead to increased material costs, increased raw materials, poor utilization of capital, and a host of other negative consequences. Considering the situation where there is a demand rate greater than 5 units per hour, operating the first operation at a sustained rate greater than 5 units per hour will build work-in-process inventory between operation 1 and operation 2 with no subsequent increase in profitability. This situation is unfavorable because the organization is tying up its money on activities and inventories that do not lead to increased profitability. There is no positive bottom-line impact in this situation.

Consider the following example: During a plant tour, the plant manager went out of his way to show and discuss his prize possession—an absolutely huge multimillion-dollar piece of equipment. It took a number of operators to run it, and the whole plant operated around this one piece of equipment. The objective of this plant was to feed this monster and have it spit out product at the other end. One of the team leaders proudly mentioned how the piece of equipment was a contributor to the local economy by creating the need for high-tech, high-paying jobs. A walk to the finishing area, however, revealed excess inventory everywhere, some of which had been around for a good bit of time. With all of this inventory lying around, it was easy to wonder whether the monster was creating jobs or ultimately destroying jobs. Someone somewhere must pay for the decision to run this machine six days per week without the demand for its product.

As can be seen from this example, such actions can lead to poorer performance. Assume, for instance, that each unit sells for $5.00 and that the material cost is $2.00. Over the period of one day, if operation 1 is run at 100 percent efficiency and utilization the net flow rate in Equation 7.20 is determined by the number of units sold at $5.00 over the analysis period and the amount spent on materials. The first operation consumes materials at a rate of $20.00 per hour. Over an eight-hour day, this is $160.00. Since revenue is generated at the rate of $25.00 per hour, over an entire day, this translates into $200.00 in revenue. Thus, for an entire day, the organization makes $40.00.

$$\text{Money}_{j+1} = \text{Money}_j + \text{Net Flow Rate}_j \qquad (7.20)$$

Equation 7.21 suggests that the organization has $40.00 more than it had the previous period. What would have happened if operation 1 produced only what was required of it—namely, five units per hour? Material costs would have been half of what they were. This means that over the course of a day, material costs would be $80.00 rather than $160.00 (Equation 7.22).

$$\text{Money}_{j+1} = \text{Money}_j + \$40.00 \qquad (7.21)$$

$$\text{Money}_{j+1} = \text{Money}_j + \$120.00 \qquad (7.22)$$

By lowering utilization and/or efficiency, the organization is more profitable, for it now makes $80.00 more per day. There is less risk because there is less concern for obsolete inventory. The organization has extra money that it can invest in moneymaking ventures rather than pieces of steel laying around. Reducing the cost per unit of operation 1 means nothing if the organization is losing money.

Another problem would be the following: Assume that after two days of operating at 100 percent efficiency and 100 percent utilization, another order for 50 units of a different design, higher priority, and higher CRR comes in. Between operation 1 and operation 2, there would be 80 units of work in process. Operation 2 has two days worth of work before it can get to the second order. As the buffer size gets larger, the second operation begins processing the order later, which, in turn, increases the lead time for the second order. Lead time is a function of work-in-process inventory. Larger inventories lead to longer lead times, which leads to longer promise dates and fewer opportunities for value pricing. Increased sales and competitive position can often be enhanced by shorter lead times. Arbitrarily enforcing unnecessarily high efficiency and utilization measures can increase work-in-process inventory, which leads to a process that is less profitable and less competitive.

The organization in this case is better off by operating at lower efficiencies and utilization for operation 1. Efficiency and utilization should be a function of what is necessary given the capability of the production system and the demand placed on it. For example, it could be suggested for this system that operation 1 should be required to maintain two hours of processing inventory for operation 2 in order to maximize profitability by maximizing the difference between revenues and costs. Cost minimization would occur through managing inventory, and revenue maximization would occur by ensuring that the second operation is never starved for parts and is at maximum efficiency and utilization. In this case, the machine in operation 1 might be utilized approximately 50 percent of the time. The expected output would be five parts per hour. This creates an environment where work-in-process inventory is managed and throughput is maximized.

In the case where work-in-process inventory is lower, the second operation can begin processing in two hours rather than two days. This allows for the marketing group to quote shorter lead times, which can lead to increased business and, therefore, increased sales. To operate in this environment, the responsibility of operation 1 would be to maintain the two-hour buffer—a technique used in the pull-oriented JIT but not in the push-oriented mass production. Therefore, utilization would not be an important measure at all, and efficiency would be based on maintaining the two-hour buffer with stiff penalties for not maintaining it effectively.

Regarding the situation where the market demand is less than five units per hour, the organization has two responsibilities. The first would be to meet demand with the minimal cost. The revenues would be limited, so to maintain or increase profitability, cost management becomes the issue. Assume, for instance, that the demand is for three units of production rather than five. Operation 2 can operate at a sustained rate of three units per hour. Operation 1 is required to sustain a predetermined time buffer of, say, 1.5 hours of production for operation 2. In this case, the profitability would be determined by the rate of sales, which is $15.00 per hour, and the rate of incurring costs, which would be approximately $6.00 per hour. On an hourly basis, the optimal profit would be $9.00 per hour. Now, assume that the organization did not deviate from the production schedule with the two-hour time buffer. Although this scenario was desirable when demand exceeded supply, it is now much less than optimal. The material usage rate is $10.00 per hour, while the revenue rate is still $15.00 per hour. The profitability is now $5.00 per hour when running operation 2 at 100 percent.

The second responsibility of the organization should be to look to increase the profitability of the system either by outsourcing the capacity by taking advantage of its core competencies (outsourcing high-precision machining capabilities, for example) or by reducing the resource costs (for instance, laying off workers).

OPERATION BALANCING

The purpose of an individual machine or process is to support the remaining machines that make up the process or processes that make up the system, respectively. In a manufacturing environment, the purpose is to produce high-quality products in a timely fashion—not to operate machines. As was shown previously, unnecessarily running a machine actually leads to the reduced profitability of the organization.

The role of each operation in a process is to help maximize the difference between revenues and costs over a predetermined time period. Therefore, given the fact that one operation is faster, it will have idle time that corresponds, in magnitude, to its capability relative to the parts of the process it must support. Companies must accept this. Balancing the assembly line is not necessary for the sake of reduced costs and might, in fact, be detrimental to the system. Due to issues of statistical fluctuations and dependent events, an organization might find it more difficult to recover from incidents in the manufacturing process.[19] This is a very important issue because the inability of the system to rebound from delays caused by everything from late shipments to machine breakdowns leads to lower profits and much higher lead times.

Consider the following example. An organization has a two-step process with the first operation capable of processing at j units per hour and the second operation capable of processing at k units per hour (Exhibit 7.2). There is a buffer equal to n hours of processing for the second operation. In other words, if the second operation processed at a rate of 5 units per hour and there was a time buffer of two hours, there would be 10 units in the buffer. Assume further that $j > k$. The role of the first operation is to maintain the buffer size to ensure that delays early in the process do not affect the second operation (assuming that the demand is greater than the supply).

The rate of change of the buffer, found in Equation 7.23, is equal to the difference between the rate of units going into the buffer and the rate of units leaving the buffer.

$$\frac{\Delta \text{Buffer Size}}{\text{Hour}} = j - k \qquad (7.23)$$

If the difference between j and k is large, the buffer will either be depleted or increased more rapidly than if there is a small difference. For example, if $j = 100$ and $k = 1$, the buffer, with processes operating at 100 percent, will increase at 99 units per hour.

What happens if operation 1 goes down for m hours? The buffer size is now $n - m$ hours. The objective of the first operation is to build up the buffer. If a three-hour buffer is depleted by one hour because operation 1 was not available, the first operation must replace, in the buffer, the equivalent of one hour of production for the second operation. The expression for determining just how

Exhibit 7.2   Example of a Production System with Arbitrary
              Operating Rates

| Operation 1 | Operation 2 |
| j units/hour | k units/hour |

many units must be produced is found in Equation 7.24. Simply multiply the operating rate of operation 2 by the amount of time that operation 1 was down, m, to determine the total number of units consumed during that time.

$$Y = mk \qquad (7.24)$$

How long does it take for operation 1 to make Y units? Well, if the total number of replacement parts is equal to 20 and operation 1 operates at a rate of 10 units per hour, it might be assumed that it would take two hours. This is not a correct assumption, however. Operation 2 is still running. If it operates at 5 units per hour, the net rate of increase for the buffer is only 5 units per hour (Equation 7.25). Operation 1 would need four hours and not two.

$$T = \frac{Y}{j - k}$$
$$= \frac{20}{10 - 5}$$
$$= 4 \qquad (7.25)$$

What happens as j and k approach each other? What if their values were closer in magnitude? As suggested by Equation 7.26, the time necessary to refill the buffer approaches infinity as the operating rates approach each other. Will two operations operating at exactly the same rate ever be able to build a buffer between them? No.

$$\lim_{k \to j} T = \lim_{k \to j} \frac{Y}{j - k} = \qquad (7.26)$$

Thus, if operation 1 goes down again, the situation becomes worse. Operation 2 also will go down, leading to a situation where revenues are lost (costs do *not* increase), which leads, in turn, to suboptimal financial performance. An organization could ensure maximum throughput of this system over time by considering a very large buffer size. This will increase cost and lead time, which, in turn, leads to less competitive conditions.

Still, measures exist that emphasize line balancing. As suggested by Groover, balance delay measures line efficiency, which results from idle time due to imperfect allocation of work among stations.[20] To flexibly balance by adjusting utilization and efficiency is not a bad thing. To force balancing, as some have suggested in the past, by adjusting the natural throughput capabilities of operations in a process might create a suboptimal operating environment.

Does this discussion hold true if demand is less than supply capability? Yes, it does; however, the result might not be as critical. It is possible to have a depleted buffer, which causes the second operation to go down. This is acceptable as long as the existing demand is met. If, however, through balancing, the buffer cannot be filled and operation 2 is starved to the point where it cannot meet demand, the organization will, again, see suboptimal financial performance.

Endnotes

[1]See, for example, Robert H. Hayes and Steven C. Wheelwright, *Restoring Our Competitive Edge: Competing Through Manufacturing* (New York: John Wiley & Sons, 1984).

[2]Taking the logarithm of both sides, Equation 4.4 becomes $\ln P_i = \ln P_1 + r \ln i$. This equation has the form of $y = b + mx$, with m being the slope of the line.

[3]Hayes and Wheelwright, *Restoring Our Competitive Edge*, p. 234.

[4]Hayes and Wheelwright, *Restoring Our Competitive Edge*, p. 54.

[5]Hayes and Wheelwright, *Restoring Our Competitive Edge*, p. 55.

[6]Hayes and Wheelwright, *Restoring Our Competitive Edge*, p. 58.

[7]Elsayed A. Elsayed and Thomas O. Boucher, *Analysis and Control of Production Systems* (Englewood Cliffs, NJ: Prentice Hall, 1985), p. 63.

[8]Elsayed and Boucher, *Analysis and Control of Production Systems*, p. 61.

[9]Kamlesh Mathur and Daniel Solow, *Management Science: The Art of Decision Making* (Englewood Cliffs, NJ: Prentice Hall, 1994).

[10]Mathur and Solow, Management Science.

[11]Eliyahu M. Goldratt and Robert E. Fox, *The Race* (Croton-on-Hudson, NY: North River Press, 1986).

[12]Mathur & Solow, *Management Science*, p. 592.

[13]Joseph G. Monks, *Theory and Problems of Operations Management* (New York: Schaum's Outline Series, McGraw-Hill, 1985), p. 240.

[14]Barry Render and Ralph M. Stair, Jr., *Quantitative Analysis for Management* (Needham Heights, MA: Allyn and Bacon, 1994), p. 286.

[15]Mathur and Solow, *Management Science*, pp. 593–95.

[16]Mathur and Solow, *Management Science*, p. 594.

[17]Shiqeo Shingo, *A Revolution in Manufacturing: the SMED System*. trans. Andrew P. Dillon (1993: reprint, Boston: Productivity Press, 1985)

[18]See, for example, Goldratt and Fox, *The Race*.

[19]See, for example, Umble & Srikanth. M. Michael Umble & ML Srikanth, *Synchronous Manufacturing: Principles for World Class Excellence*. (Cincinnati: South-Western Publishing, 1990.)

[20]Groover (1987), p. 147.

8

Resource and Program Management

Thus far, the concept of explicit cost dynamics (ECD), as well as costs and their multidisciplinary nature, have been introduced. In addition, you have read about cost levels and cost types, new cost management measures, applied this knowledge to profit dynamics, and in the previous chapter, learned common management myths. This chapter, which focuses on how to apply this knowledge to manage resources and programs, will begin with a discussion of resource costs. The focus will be on creating a picture of how to effectively manage resource costs, and the discussion will then shift to program costs. Internally facing and externally facing programs will be discussed, and examples of each will be introduced and discussed. As you review this chapter, remember that this is not a management book; it is a book about costs and cost dynamics. The suggestions in this chapter and in the remaining chapters will focus on how management actions affect the cost dynamics of the situation. As firms find unique ways of applying the principles, leading practices hopefully will be shared among all.

RESOURCE COSTS

Resource costs are the costs that a company would incur if all actions stopped—if no phone calls were made, no products were built or delivered, no services were provided, and no items were purchased. From the traditional economics perspective, resource costs would include land, labor, and capital.

Land partially owned or rented by the company also is a resource cost, for the company must pay for this land whether it is used or not. The lease payments are ongoing; for as long as there are terms to the agreement, the lease payments must be made. Therefore, the lease payments themselves will show up on the bottom line as resource costs. Warehouses and offices create an interesting dilemma for cost accountants. If an organization leases warehouse space, that space is a nonallocable cost. Office space, similarly, is nonallocable. However, traditional costing techniques would suggest that the organization could allocate the cost of the space to those using the space.

Assume, for example, that there are two products being stored in a warehouse. The monthly payments may be allocated to both products based on drivers such as space utilization. If one product takes up 70 percent of the space, for instance, it would absorb 70 percent of the lease payment. If the organization decides to cut back on the number of product A that is kept in the warehouse, the potential exists for an increase in the cost of product B because product A now takes up a smaller percentage of the whole. Office-space allocation can behave the same way. If one department decides to change the space that it uses, the implementation of the decision could lead to increases in costs for other departments. Understand, however, that the costs associated with producing product B are the same. What sense does it make to increase the cost of product B even though the lease payments remain the same? Allocating these costs does not affect the bottom line and could increase the cost of the product to the point where the margins might be undesirable. No department or product should suffer the burden of decisions made that are independent of its own fate.

Thus, to avoid this situation, the cost of the space should not be allocated. The company will have the cost of the space whether it is used or not. Instead of devising sophisticated costing algorithms, define the costs as resource costs and focus on the effective management of the resources.

Labor is another resource cost. Direct labor historically has been considered a variable cost. However, if the definition of a variable cost in a manufacturing environment is based on the number of units produced and if direct labor workers are paid based on the number of hours worked, there is a disconnect: The workers being paid by the hour or any other time period are going to be paid whether they make their standard production, exceed it, or fail to achieve it. The workers will be paid regardless of output, and the impact on the bottom line of the labor will always remain the same. The only exception to direct labor being a resource cost is if the labor is paid based on piecework rather than time; that is, the more pieces that they make, the more that they are paid. Other than paying workers for actual production, to assume that labor costs are variable is meaningless.

Similarly, indirect labor is a resource cost. Recall the example in Chapter 6 where the allocation of indirect labor was considered. By allocating the indirect labor through the burden factor, a situation is created in which it can be assumed that indirect labor varies with production as well. To assume that indirect labor changes with production time or rate is a meaningless exercise. The cost of production control, the time of the partners in a partnership, and the time that an accountant spends trying to make indirect costs vary all are resource costs and are completely independent of the number of units that are produced or the number of services that are provided. In fact, if direct labor is independent of the number of units that are produced, why is indirect labor not independent?

How, then, does an organization measure the effectiveness of labor? How effective and efficient labor is should be determined by efficiency and effectiveness measures of the labor. The efficiency of the resource should be measured by how effectively the resource is being utilized. There are two ways of measuring how effectively a resource is being utilized. First, look at the resource action list. What is the resource involved in? Does the resource have time to play solitaire, or is the resource working overtime to make ends meet? Being busy is not enough, however. The second measure focuses on considering the programs with which a resource is involved. If a resource is a valuable contributor to a number of programs that in some way add value to the organization or if the programs in which the resource is involved are required by the government or by customers, management might want to rank the resource highly. If the resource is not highly utilized or if the resource is not involved with value-added activities, the organization must question the need and use of the resource. Clearly, there should be a sliding scale. The organization cannot expect a newly graduated engineer, for example, to add the same value that an experienced engineer can. This is an issue for management to address. The key issue is to focus on the contributions that resources make and how they enable bottom-line impacts (BLIs).

Capital is the third type of resource cost. For the sake of simplicity, assume that capital is what the company owns or is buying and can liquidate. Given this definition, machines, inventory, and information systems owned by the company are all considered resource costs. Payments for a machine will exist regardless of what is produced by that machine. In fact, if nothing is produced, the lease payment still exists. Also, the lease payment remains the same if the machine makes an infinite number of products. The one surprise here is inventory. Why is inventory a resource cost? It depends. Why the organization purchased or created the inventory is the most important question. Organizations purchase items for two reasons. The first reason is that the item is purchased because it is filling existing demand. For example, a customer approaches the organization and asks the organization to fill a need that it has, such as to build a house or to sell a pencil. Either way, if the organization chooses to fill the order, it is likely that it will have to buy something. If the organization buys the necessary items specifically for the purpose of filling the order, the cost of the items is not considered a resource cost. In this case, the costs are item costs. If a company must buy a special window for a house that it is building for a client, the cost is incurred only because of the existence of the order. It becomes an item cost that goes into the total cost of the house-building program.

The second reason, however, is quite different. If a company procures materials for which there is no order, these items are now resources. They add to the capacity of the organization to meet future orders. Organizations buy inventory so that they can be responsive to market demands, which is really no different than why a company may secure labor ahead of time. By forecasting, companies often look to the planning horizon in an attempt to determine the future demands on the organization. Based on this forecast, organizations plan their resources. How much labor capacity will be required? How much machine capacity will be required? How much material capacity will be required? The mere fact that organizations plan and procure based on this forecast suggests that production and procurement are independent. If they were totally dependent, companies would have excess inventory only in extreme cases; a case in which the company might be able to get others to foot the bill for causing the excess inventory, for example, might be a cancelled order. Otherwise, the company bets on what the future will look like, procures its resources, and hopes that its future comes through.

RESOURCE COST DYNAMICS

As previously discussed, resource costs are constant and change as steps. Consider the cost to lease warehouse space. If an organization pays $10,000.00 per month to rent warehouse space, that lease payment will remain $10,000.00 per month unless the terms of the lease dictate a change. No matter how the space is used, the payments will be the same; allocating the space will not change the lease payment, and using the space more efficiently will not change the lease payment. In the following three situations, an organization can impact what occurs for a given lease cost:

1. The company needs more space, and the options being considered are either to lease more space or to use existing space.
2. The company uses existing space effectively but wants to reduce the cost of the current space.
3. The company has too much space and wants to somehow cut costs.

Growing Need for Space

In this case, the organization finds that it is running out of warehouse space. How can the organization handle the need to store more inventory? One option is to lease more space, which obviously creates an opportunity for the company to store the inventory somewhat easily. The problem with this approach is that it increases the lease costs. So, if the additional space is $5,000.00, per month, the total warehouse space is now $15,000.00 per month. The second option is to determine if the existing space can be used more effectively so that additional space is not necessary. More effective utilization of warehouse space creates another degree of freedom. If, through more efficient utilization of warehouse space, the organization does not need to lease more warehouse space, costs have not been saved—the lease cost is still $10,000.00 per month. The action has allowed the company to do more with existing space, thus avoiding the additional costs associated with the expansion. There is, of course, another option, for companies can choose not to create or hold the inventory at all. This, however, is the subject for another book.

Improving the Status Quo

If a company is currently leasing warehouse space and is unhappy with the leasing costs, it has three options that affect the bottom line. The first option is to try to renegotiate a lower lease payment. By lowering the monthly lease payment, the organization clearly will be spending less money per month, which impacts how the lease affects the bottom line. Less money per period leaves the company. The next option, which is similar, is to move to another location with a lower lease payment. The net effect is really the same; less money is spent on a monthly basis, which clearly has a BLI. The third option is to determine how to more efficiently use the warehouse space so that less space can be rented. Using less space might create an additional degree of freedom in terms of how management wants to handle the warehouse space. Instead of renting 50,000 square feet, perhaps the organization can lease 35,000 square feet. The key word is *lease* and not *use*. If the company leases 50,000 square feet but uses 35,000 square feet, no money was saved. Only if the organization can position itself to lease less space for less money can the organization achieve a BLI.

Managing Excess Space

The third situation is that a company has too much space and wants to cut costs. What options exist for the company? Unless there are strategic reasons why the organization must keep the space, the company should consider getting rid of the excess space. Now, the company is in the same situation as the company in the second scenario that wanted to lease less space. Excess capacity may create additional degrees of freedom, which the company can use to reduce its costs.

Handling the Need for More Space

When considering the issue of managing growth, the organization should always look to create degrees of freedom. Creating degrees of freedom will allow the organization to always have at least two options. In this case, efficient warehouse space utilization allows the organization to have two options until the point where no more can be received out of the existing space. If it is suggested that the company needs more warehouse space, justify the need by considering the utilization of the existing space. This is what cost management is about. By focusing on efficient space utilization, the organization is able to maintain degrees of freedom that can help managers more effectively manage the organization. If it is shown that the organization cannot get more from the space, use the option to get more space. If there is more to get from the existing space, get it. There are, of course, limits. Anyone who has ridden in the back of a Boeing 757 across the country knows that trying to squeeze too much from a resource might create discomfort for those who have to deal with the situation!

PROGRAM COSTS

A program is the lowest level in the ECD framework to which costs can be assigned. The cost types that are assigned to programs are action costs and item costs. Recall that resource costs exist in the absence of programs; action costs and item costs are incurred for specific reasons. For example, an organization might incur material item costs because it has a program to meet the demand created by a customer order. It might also incur costs because it is trying to figure out how to reduce the costs that are incurred when trying to fill an order. For whatever reason, action and item costs should all be assigned to a program. The word *assigned* is used instead of *allocated* because of the simple fact that in the ECD framework, costs cannot be allocated. They can be incurred, and because they are incurred, they must be assigned to a program. They must be assigned to programs because organizations should have a way to manage, control, cut, or grow costs.

Programs have another reason for existence. Resource time will be assigned to programs and superprograms, which will help the organization keep track of the utilization of resources. This is important because without this information, it will be difficult to understand how resources are being utilized. Resource utilization is a measure that will be very important when it comes to managing existing capacity as well as justifying changes to current capacity. How, for instance, will an organization decide to increase its capacity if it does not have detailed enough information describing how overburdened the existing capacity is?

PROGRAM TYPES

Two types of programs exist. One is an internally facing (IF) program, which focuses on necessary operations. The other general type of program is an externally facing (EF) program, which exists to meet the demands that customers place on the organization.

Internally Facing Programs

Programs that are generally necessary to operate the organization are IF programs. An improvement is an IF program, which the organization decides to use in order to improve its operations. Programs also exist that help the organization to operate in its respective market. These programs might include activities such as product development or general and manufacturing operations in an environment where organizations build products to a forecast and store them in inventory. Finally, there are programs that are required by law, such as financial accounting, tax accounting, and legal programs. Each of these program types will be discussed in turn.

Operations Programs

Operations programs typically are used to operate the organization on a daily basis. These types of programs will always exist in organizations. The key from a cost management perspective is to manage the number and scope of each one that exists. Because of their relative importance, operations programs must exist; however, organizations must be very careful with them. Because there has been no way to measure their contribution to the organization, the justification techniques have gone relatively unchecked. Thus, it is easy for these programs to get out of hand in both number and in scope. Examples of operations programs include running the information systems group; accounting, including accounts payables and accounts receivables; human resources such as hiring, firing, and training; and item procurement.

Measuring these types of programs involves first defining the program and its scope. It is then a matter of identifying what costs will be created as a result of the program. The resources are not counted because the resources are going to exist whether the program exists or not. In foresight, the planning process should identify how the programs will operate, what actions will occur, and what items will be purchased as a result of the program. Clearly, there will be guessing, which is acceptable as long as the assumptions are documented and the owners and stakeholders agree. In hindsight, however, there is a different story. At the end of a period of time within the project or at the end of the overall program, all of the costs would be identifiable so that the organization knows exactly what the costs were. Capturing these data and comparing them to the estimates can help identify opportunities for improvement in the improvement plan and can make issues that may be related to risks and risk mitigation more salient.

Operating Program Example: Human Resources and Hiring. While in a meeting, a human resources vice president begins to talk about the cost to hire resources. There is significant concern because the cost to hire a new resource is much too high. Analyzing the costs associated with hiring a resource, some are explicit while others are not. As shown in Exhibit 8.1, only a few truly explicit costs exist, and human resources labor is not one of them.

To determine the cost to hire an individual, the organization could begin by defining a program to hire an individual. This program can capture the explicit costs incurred, and the organization can begin to understand just how expensive it is to hire someone.

To reduce costs, the organization must reduce the frequency of incurring these costs or it must focus on reducing the cost per occurrence. Additionally, identifying improvements, which will increase available capacity, can reduce the cost of having a human resources organization. This available capacity creates degrees of freedom, which allow the organization to reduce its resource costs.

Improvement Programs

Improvement programs are created to identify opportunities for improvement and to implement these programs. Examples of improvement programs are process redesign and process reengineering efforts and the implementation of quality programs. The reason these programs are placed into this category is to allow organizations to understand whether or not improvement programs are making a difference to the operations and the bottom line.

When measuring improvement programs, the organization should seek to close the loop between what is found or identified

Exhibit 8.1   Examples of Explicit Costs Incurred While Recruiting Resources

Action Costs	Item Costs
Professional finders fees	Airline tickets
Lodging	
Transportation	

and what is achieved. The organization will take resources and apply them for the sole purpose of helping the organization operate more effectively. Often, significant resources are appropriated with the intention to find improvements in how the organization operates. How many companies, for instance, solicit the help of consulting firms? How many of these companies fail to achieve the value identified by the consulting firm? Many companies do both, and equal amounts probably *know* that they did not achieve the value for which they paid dearly.

By making improvement programs a major type of program, they become more salient. First, resources are assigned to the program, which provides visibility into resource utilization. Second, the improvement efforts that have been identified are also more salient to those who manage costs and hopefully to the entire organization.

Improvement Program Example: Process-Redesign Initiative. In a process-redesign initiative, the following multiple steps are involved with managing the program:

1. The possibilities should be scoped out in advance to determine whether there is enough of an opportunity to create enhancements to the organization. This group acts like a grand jury in that it begins to make a case for what should be studied and what the improvement opportunities might be.

2. At this point, decisions should be made regarding what the program scope should be, how the program will be managed, what resources will be involved, critical success factors, and measures for success. Decisions regarding whether to use consultants or outside help are also determined. With this information, a cost-benefit analysis can be performed and a decision to move forward can be made.

3. When managing the program, it is important that all costs incurred are captured against the program. The focus is not on capturing the costs for punitive purposes. Rather, for future improvements in estimating programs and their benefits, the organization must understand where they were not as accurate as they would like. Over time, refining the programs will reduce risks and will help risk mitigation.

4. Upon completing the program, the right measures must be in place and must be understood by those who will be impacted by the measures as they perform their programs. The purpose

is to measure the effectiveness of the improvement program. Again, the desire is to circle back and determine whether the organization achieved or is on track to achieve what it set out to achieve with the program. The program team should document the progress, compare the progress to the initial assessment, and finally close the program.

Product or Service Programs

Product and service programs focus on developing what the organization will eventually sell as its products. Examples of product programs are research and development, new product development, engineering test, and the other activities and processes associated with bringing a new product to market. These programs are important to the organization because they must operate efficiently and effectively while balancing research into new areas, technologies, or techniques. This balance is very difficult to maintain. First, devoting resources to research and development is a necessity for most companies as they search for new ways to solve the problems of their existing and future consumers. They must do so while either maintaining parity or an advantage over others in the industry. Second, product programs must ensure that the organization has new products that will help sustain future operations. Finally, these groups must selectively cannibalize existing products, which may impact revenues when released but enhance and ensure future organizational viability.

Product Program Example: Product Development. The purpose of new product development is to determine what products will generate future profitable sales. This is the first step of an important process that will highly impact the cost recovery ratio of the organization's products. Therefore, it is imperative that marketing, manufacturing, and other groups that will influence and be influenced by the product are involved in its design.

Product development is a highly resource-intensive discipline. From research and development to design engineering and through prototyping and aiding with the implementation into manufacturing, the numbers are significant. In addition, a significant number of actions exist. Think, for example, about creating a prototype car. There are a significant number of actions that occur and items purchased as a result of the design and development program. Additionally, the vehicle must be tested and improved. The associated actions related to testing and improvement will have costs that are fairly significant. As with the other programs, the organization must decide whether the results of the program justify the processes used that led to the results.

With product development, speed is a key criterion along with relative simplicity of design for enhanced manufacturability and re-pairability, effective use of materials, desired product functionality, and the marketability of the products. Speed implies an effective product-development process with few, if any, low-value iterations and the ability to increase the output of the product-development re-sources. Simplicity of design aids both production and repair, which can lead to enhanced profits. Although highly manufacturable prod-ucts might not reduce costs, they can increase efficiency and effec-tiveness, which leads to the opportunity to produce and, therefore, to sell more. Repairability makes ease and cost of ownership reasons for buying the organization's product. Effective use of materials helps keep the program and resource costs down. In other words, use the right materials at the right cost to ensure that clients get what they want, expect, and pay for. This does not presuppose that the or-ganization uses the latest and best materials. It should use what makes sense given its strategy and where its products fit in the mar-ket. Product functionality and marketability really do go together. Engineers provide function to enhance the user experience, which hopefully leads to a product that is easy to market and sell.

It is important to note that it is impossible to recover the costs associated with product development. Assume, for example, that product development has resource costs of $1,000,000.00 for one year. The total of the action and the item costs are $250,000.00 for the same year. By the time the product is introduced, these costs are sunk. There is absolutely nothing that the organization can do about these costs. If, during the next year, the organization utilizes the re-sources at the same rate and performs actions at the same rate, sales must recover the current product-development costs. In other words, products designed now must sell enough to sustain the existence of product development and other disciplines into the future. Allocat-ing costs of something that is not recoverable makes no sense.

Required Programs

Required programs are comprised of those actions and items that are required of the organization by law. The organization cannot do anything about the requirements placed on them; for example, they must file taxes. They must be able to develop and interpret contracts, and many organizations must file and report on their financials. Therefore, given that the activities must occur, how does the organization manage the activities from an ECD perspective?

The organization should determine which of the required programs must be owned by the organization. For example, does the organization need to have its own legal staff? Can it buy some or most of its legal services? Does the organization need to have its own financial accounting group or can the organization buy the accounting services? If these services can be purchased from the outside, the organization should weigh the benefits of owning the resources and incurring all of the actions and items associated with the required program versus buying the entire service from external sources. It may or may not just be an issue of comparing transaction costs to coordinating costs. There may be intangible benefits that will keep the organization from outsourcing the program. In the case where the organization must own the service and the cost to transact the services is lower than the cost to coordinate the services, the organization must show that the intangibles are worth at least as much as the difference in costs. Otherwise, the organization has reduced its profits unjustifiably by maintaining the higher cost option.

Required Program Example: Legal. Many firms have their own legal capacity. This legal group may handle activities ranging from handling contracts to handling external legal matters. If the legal capacity is already owned by the organization, legal programs cost nothing from a resource point of view unless temporary labor is used. Therefore, the only costs involved are the costs of phone calls, hiring reporters, travel, court, duplicating, shipping, and other related explicit costs. It should be relatively simple to document the costs involved and to associate them with the program. From this perspective, the difficulty is in handling the legal capacity itself. Should the organization own the legal services or should it outsource this capacity? A detailed analysis should be performed before agreeing to outsource this capacity. This detailed analysis must include identification of the assumptions, the intangibles associated with giving away what may be deep tacit knowledge of the organization, and a plan for reducing the resource costs after the work is outsourced.

Internally Facing Program Cost Dynamics

In each of the four types of programs, the cost dynamics are basically the same:

1. They are all composed of action and item costs only. These are the only real costs that are incurred when the organization chooses to implement a program. Everything else is a resource cost that will exist in the absence of the program.
2. They adhere to the law of conservation of dollars. Costs to the organization increase when performing an action more than once or when buying more items. Similarly, as the price of a single action or item increases, costs will go up. Costs are only identified as they leave the organization.
3. They are multidimensional in nature. In total, they will make up the costs that the products or services must recover to ensure overall profitability. If a program has more than one cost type or multiple components of a single cost type, the costs are now entering into a multidimensional space. A traditional two-dimensional analysis should be replaced by an understanding of the cost dynamics in a multi-dimensional space.

Externally Facing Programs

Programs used to seek customers and consumers and to develop and deliver their desired product or service are called EF programs. Marketing, sales, certain manufacturing functions, and various consulting groups responsible for generating revenues are all EF programs. From a cost dynamics perspective, nothing is different than IF programs; these programs will still have items and actions. The difference is in how they are measured from a profit dynamics perspective, for the goal is to have the EF programs generating revenues. Because they generate revenues, the first objective is to ensure that these programs are generating more revenue than it costs the organization to fund them. A sales group, for example, must sell more than the costs generated by its sales activities. Beyond capturing the program costs, the margin from the program can now be used to recover the organization operating costs. There are two main benefits to this approach. The first benefit is that the organization will still have the relevant information to determine the pricing of its products without artificially inflating the price by allocating costs that are truly independent. The second benefit is that the organization will have a better understanding of the investment of its externally facing programs. The programs must be profitable for the organization to be profitable. Sales must also generate enough revenues overall to pay off the operating costs that exist. To gain this level of information, the appropriate bottom-line measures must be used.

$$\text{Profit} = \Sigma \text{ Revenues}_{\text{Period}} - \Sigma \text{ Total Costs}_{\text{Period}} \qquad (8.1)$$

To develop the measures that are used for EF programs, begin with the profit equation (Equation 8.1) as was suggested in Chapter 5. All ECD measures are derived directly from the bottom line. If an organization were to look at a single EF program, it would need to ensure that the program itself is profitable. To accomplish this, the break-even point for the program must be determined.

$$\text{Program Margin} = \text{Revenue}_{\text{EF}}$$
$$- (\Sigma \text{ Action Costs}_{\text{EF}} + \Sigma \text{ Item Costs}_{\text{EF}}) \qquad (8.2)$$

$$\text{Revenue}_{\text{Breakeven}} =$$
$$\Sigma \text{ Action Costs}_{\text{Breakeven}} + \Sigma \text{ Item Costs}_{\text{Breakeven}} \qquad (8.3)$$

Breakeven will occur when the costs are offset by the revenues. To determine when this happens, begin with Equation 8.2. Recall that this equation defined the program margin, which was simply the difference in costs and revenues for a program. At breakeven for the program, the revenues and costs are equal (Equation 8.3).

Equation 8.3 would be used to assess where the organization is on a break-even surface. Cost functions are multidimensional, so one curve in two-dimensional space will often not be sufficient to represent the cost dynamics. For programs with only one action and one item to be purchased in varying quantities, a three-dimensional space would be required since the item costs and the action costs are likely to be independent. If more dimensions are required, two options are available for representing the cost dynamics. One option, likely the more tedious, is to hold one variable constant and plot the variables that can be represented in two-dimensional or three-dimensional space. For example, an organization can choose to hold constant an action cost and show the variability of the item costs in a conceivable space. This method is tedious because the organization would have to repeat the representation for varying levels of the action costs. The other method is to view the actual data to understand the cost position for varying levels of the cost variables. While this sounds complicated (and it is) it is not so difficult to conceive. Since cost functions are linear monotonically increasing functions, organizations know that the more that they do or buy, the more it is going to cost and at what rate the cost will increase. Therefore, performing a marginal analysis by changing a variable slightly will create easily predictable results. With data processing capabilities as they are, simple queries can help organizations understand where they are from a cost perspective in any n-dimensional space and then begin to make changes based on where they are on the surface.

Therefore, breakeven occurs where the revenue curve intersects the cost surface in n-space. While the basic rules are the same, how the program costs are calculated happens to be a bit more complicated. When the value of the cost function is less than the value for the revenue function, the program is profitable. When the value of the cost function is greater, the program is not profitable (Equation 8.4).

$$\text{Revenues} > \Sigma \text{ Costs} \equiv \text{Profitable}$$
$$\text{Revenues} < \Sigma \text{ Costs} \equiv \text{Unprofitable} \qquad (8.4)$$

It is extremely important to recognize the obvious here. As long as the revenues for the program exceed the activity and item costs that generated the revenues, the organization is more profitable. This seems obvious but is rarely practiced. How many organizations, for example, believe that they have to make their margins on a product to be profitable? The cost portion of the margin usually has allocated costs associated with it, suggesting that the perceived cost to be profitable is often higher than the actual cost.

Profit Stages

The program break-even point will occur when the margin for a program is equal to zero. At a value below zero, the costs exceed the revenues and, therefore, the company is losing money. This is different than a traditional break-even analysis because the resource costs and IF programs are not considered. The reason they are not considered when analyzing breakeven for the program is that they are independent of the costs incurred by the program. However, to assess the profitability of the organization as a whole, resource costs and IF programs must be considered because total cost is one key variable in determining overall profitability. Recall that there are really two break-even points: one is for the program, and the other is for the organization. Although they were introduced in Chapter 5, the levels of profitability are repeated here for simplicity (Exhibit 8.2).

Exhibit 8.2   There Are Five Stages of Profitability, Which Include
Two Break-even Points

Stage	Condition	Meaning
1	CRR < 0	Unprofitable program
2	CRR = 0	Program breakeven
3	0 < CRR < 1	Program profitable below traditional breakeven
4	CRR = 1	Traditional breakeven
5	CRR > 1	Profitable operation

Exhibit 8.3   The Program Margin Helps Assess Whether a Program
Is Profitable

Program Margin	Meaning
<0	Program is unprofitable
0	Program breaks even
>0	Program is profitable and contributes positively to the bottom line

The first three stages of profitability are focused on the program itself. The key is to recognize the contribution that the program makes to overall profitability (Exhibit 8.3). In most cases, one program will not cover all of an organization's operating costs. This does not mean that the program does not contribute to paying off the organization operating costs.

As shown in Exhibit 8.2, there are five stages to achieving profitability:

1. *Not profitable.* The program revenues will not recover the program costs. The organization operating costs remain the same, but the total costs are increasing at a rate faster than the revenues received, thus leading to a perpetually unprofitable situation.

2. *Program breakeven.* In general, the company is no worse off than if it had not taken on the work. The bills from the program are paid. However, the organization operating costs are not and will not be recovered at this rate.

3. *Program profitable.* Since the program is profitable, it is paying off a portion of the organization operating costs. However, the

organization operating costs are usually not totally recovered. Therefore, the company might not be profitable in total, but the resources are being paid at a rate faster than the costs are being incurred.

4. *Aggregate breakeven.* Aggregate breakeven occurs when the total costs, including organization operating costs and the total revenues, are equal. This is comparable to the traditional break-even point.

5. *Aggregate profitability.* When the organization operating costs have been recovered and the program margin is positive, the company is beyond its aggregate break-even point and, therefore, is profitable on the bottom line.

In addition to bottom-line profitability, a measure that helps organizations determine where they are in terms of overall profitability and how well an EF program contributes financially is the cost recovery ratio, or the CRR. The CRR (introduced in Chapter 5) is simply an expression that helps managers know what percentage of the organization operating costs has been recovered by a program after its own program costs have been taken out (Equation 8.5). This helps the organization understand the contribution to overall profitability of an EF program. Note that the numerator of Equation 8.5 is the program margin (PM). Therefore, Equation 8.5 can be simplified and represented as the ratio of the PM and the organization operating costs, as shown in Equation 8.6.

$$CRR = \frac{Revenue_{Specific\ Program} - (\Sigma\ Action\ Costs_{Specific\ Program} + \Sigma\ Item\ Costs_{Specific\ Program})}{Organization\ Operating\ Cost}$$

(8.5)

$$CRR_{Program} = \frac{PM}{Organization\ Operating\ Cost}$$

$$CRR_{Aggregate} = \frac{\Sigma\ PM}{Organization\ Operating\ Cost}$$

(8.6)

From Equation 8.6, the relationship between the PM, the CRR, and the profit stage becomes more easily apparent. With the PM being in the numerator, whenever the PM is positive, the CRR will be positive, suggesting that the organization is recovering its operating costs. When the CRR is greater than 1, the organization is profitable in aggregate (Exhibit 8.4).

Exhibit 8.4 Determining the CRR and the PM Helps Identify the
            Profit Stage of the Organization

Profit Stage	Stage Name	Description	Program Margin	CRR
1	Not profitable	Program and company are both not profitable	<0	<0
2	Program breakeven not profitable	Program has broken even but resource costs cannot be paid	=0	=0
3	Program level profitable but not profitable in aggregate	Program is profitable and begins to pay off resources although they have not been recovered	>0	<1
4	Aggregate breakeven	All costs, including resource costs, have been recovered exactly	>0	=1
5	Aggregate profitability	Resource costs have all been recovered	>0	>1

The CRR is different in the value it provides for organizations than traditional profit margins. It demonstrates how quickly product or *program* sales recover the organization operating costs. The CRR can be used as a measurement to determine prices or even whether certain programs should be taken on at all. If the organization operating costs for a period and the program costs are known and if a predetermined CRR has been obtained, program margins and, thus, prices can be determined. In the case where an organization is bidding on prices, the only unknown might be the market price. If all costs are known and the company has a minimum CRR that it would like to meet, the price can be subsequently determined from the CRR.

Externally Facing Program Example: Manufacturing. Assume that a company makes two products, A and B. Exhibit 8.5 represents the information regarding costs and revenues. Assume for the sake of simplicity that the production process is one machine, operation, or process, and other costs (utilities, for example) will be ignored. The action costs in this case are a result of the materials that are scrapped as part of shifting production from either product A to product B or vice versa. The purpose of this analysis is to show how

Exhibit 8.5   Data for Cost Example

	Product A	Product B
Item cost ($/unit)	$ 10	$ 20
Action cost (setup waste)	$200	$400
Revenues ($/unit)	$ 20	$ 35

an organization would use the PM and to compare it to contribution margin and full-absorption costing. As a result, it will be determined that the PM is superior to contribution margins and full absorption in two ways. First, an organization will know into which particular profit scenario a price will place the program. What difference, for example, will a $2.00 price have on the profit stage of the company versus a $5.00 price? The difference is significant because unless the program is of strategic importance, stage one should be avoided altogether. Stage two requires resources that can be used on other programs that might lead to stage three higher levels of profitability. Taking on this type of work should be of highly strategic importance.

Companies should attempt to price programs into stage three at a minimum, for this would ensure that the resources are being paid with each program. The other types of costing do not provide such detailed information, and not knowing this information might lead to pricing that is actually detrimental to the financial performance of the company. Another benefit of PM pricing is its flexibility. Program margins do not tell the organization at what price a program and its output should be priced. Instead, it provides important answers to questions such as the following:

- What would happen if the price were x?
- What should the price be to ensure the program is at profitability stage three?
- Can the company accept a price of y and still be at stage two at a minimum?

Back to the example, begin by determining the break-even value for the program, Equation 8.2 would be applied. For product A, the break-even number of units is 20 units sold at a price of $20.00 (Equation 8.7). As shown in Equation 8.8, at $35.00, the breakeven for product B is 27 units sold (it is usually not possible to sell 1/3 of a unit). Any number of units sold greater than the break-even quantity will create a positive PM and CRR.

$$0 = \$20.00 \ (\text{Units}) - [\$10.00 \ (\text{Units}) + \$200.00]$$
$$= \$10.00 \ (\text{Units}) - \$200.00$$
$$\$10.00 \ (\text{Units}) = \$200.00$$
$$\text{Units} = 20 \qquad\qquad (8.7)$$

$$0 = \$35.00 \ (\text{Units}) - [\$20.00 \ (\text{Units}) + \$400.00]$$
$$= \$15.00 \ (\text{Units}) - \$400.00$$
$$\$15.00 \ (\text{Units}) = \$400.00$$
$$\text{Units} = 26.66 = 27 \qquad\qquad (8.8)$$

Contribution Margin Costing

Consider the contribution margin approach, which suggests that profitable pricing occurs when revenues exceed variable costs. The rationale is that when revenues are larger than the extra costs incurred in creating those revenues, fixed costs can be reduced by using the difference to pay them off. Conceptually, it is very close to the PM; however, this approach does not consider action costs. Therefore, when using the contribution margin approach in this example, as long as the company is producing and selling parts, it is operating profitably. The program breakeven is actually zero units for contribution margin values greater than or equal to zero. As long as the company produces, it is recovering its fixed costs. By not considering action costs, however, the contribution margin can actually be positive while the company is losing money producing the product. In this example, neglecting setup costs, for example, creates a situation where the company believes that it can produce, say, 10 units and that it can be profitable doing so. As seen in Exhibit 8.6, this assumption is incorrect.

If the organization were to allocate the setup cost as a variable cost, the result for contribution margins actually turns out to be the same as for program margins; however, this defeats the purpose of contribution costing. If the organization were to allocate the setup costs, why not allocate other costs as well? Although the math allows the same solution under some circumstances, it is the resultant thinking in this case that is of concern. By allocating setup costs, the limiting unit cost thinking is utilized rather than the total profit thinking. Although the cost per unit does, in fact,

Exhibit 8.6   Comparing Contribution Margin to Program Margin

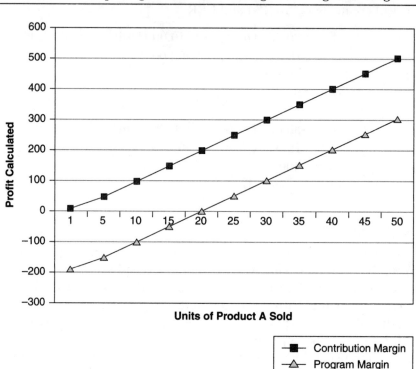

go down, the company is more profitable because it is getting more revenues for the same action cost. The emphasis should be on profit and the decisions that maximize profit rather than on minimizing costs.

Absorption Costing

Using absorption costing, it is only important to know what, specifically, the overhead burden rate is so that it can be allocated to determine the program break-even point. Assume, for the sake of simplicity, that the direct labor hour rate is $10.00 and that the burden rate is 1.5. Also assume that product A requires one hour of operating time while product B requires three hours. The variable cost (VC), determined by first assuming that labor varies with production, is found by summing the material and labor costs for one unit (Equation 8.9).

$$VC_A = \text{Material Cost} + \text{Labor Cost}$$
$$= \text{Material Cost} + [\text{Direct Labor} + 1.5(\text{Direct Labor})] \times$$
$$\text{Production Time Per Unit}$$
$$= \$10.00 + \$10.00 \text{ :ts } (2.5) \times 1$$
$$= \$35.00 \tag{8.9}$$

$$VC_B = \$20.00 + \$10.00 \times (2.5) \times 3$$
$$= \$95.00 \tag{8.10}$$

According to this technique, the organization must sell product A at a price of over $35.00 to be profitable, while product B must be sold at a price of $95.00 to be profitable (Equation 8.10). The only legitimate aspect of this method lies with the fact that it tries to consider the overhead in order to determine cost and therefore price. A product would not be sold, for example, if it could not recover the overhead costs. The first concern, however, is with the fact that *the method does not provide correct information regarding pricing information and the effects on overall profitability.* For example, in this case, the company might make the decision to produce two of product B for a price of $110.00 each. This should provide the company with $15.00 profit for each unit and should allow the company to operate profitably. However, looking at the PM perspective proves otherwise (Equation 8.11).

$$PM = \$220.00 - (\$40.00 + \$400.00)$$
$$= \$220.00 - (\$440.00)$$
$$= -\$220.00 < 0 \text{ Unprofitable} \tag{8.11}$$

In this case, the company believes that it is profitable. It can sell the items at $110.00 each and make money. However, the PM suggests that the company did not even recover its costs for this particular program. The result is that the company is operating less profitably than it believed it was, a very dangerous situation. If large enough in magnitude or if sustained for long periods, for example, operating less profitably can lead to going out of business. An interesting note is, if asked to sell seven products at $80.00 each, the organization might assume that it will not make its margins and, therefore, might choose not to sell its product at that price. The PM, however, tells a different story (Equation 8.12).

$$PM = \$560.00 - (\$140.00 + \$400.00)$$
$$= \$560.00 - (\$540.00)$$
$$= \$20.00 > 0 \text{ Profitable} \tag{8.12}$$

Another concern with this approach is that of pricing. It is easy to see that a company using improper costing techniques can end up pricing its products improperly. Full absorption, for example, would suggest that the price should be some number greater than $95.00 regardless of the number of units. The program margin technique would suggest that for the two units in this case, the price should be determined as shown in Equation 8.13.

$$0 < 2 \times \text{Price} - (\$40.00 + \$400.00)$$
$$0 < 2 \times \text{Price} - (\$440.00)$$
$$\$440.00 < 2 \times \text{Price}$$
$$\$220.00 < \text{Price} \tag{8.13}$$

Similarly, for 30 units,

$$0 < 30 \times \text{Price} - (\$600.00 + \$400.00)$$
$$0 < 30 \times \text{Price} - (\$1,000.00)$$
$$\$1,000.00 < 30 \times \text{Price}$$
$$\$33.33 < \text{Price} \tag{8.14}$$

The price to ensure program breakeven, then, will decrease as the number of units is increased (Exhibit 8.7).

Absorption costing leads to an incorrect understanding of the financial impact of decisions.[1] This incorrect understanding can lead to lower profits than an organization is capable of achieving. The organization can incorrectly price its products, for instance. Incorrect pricing can be in the form of pricing products or services unknowingly too high with the intention of obtaining desired margins. This is positive as long as the organization is not pricing itself out of markets unnecessarily. Incorrect pricing can also be in the form of assuming certain margins are being obtained and, therefore, lower prices are established. If prices are too low, the company might be operating at stage two or, even worse, stage one.

The organization in this example is better off using the PM approach because of the importance of the information that is received. True, a margin for each program can be determined; however, the PM considers more data regarding what is involved with making a certain program than does contribution margins. With regard to absorption costing, the assumptions necessary to make it work might lead to behavior that undermines the system.

To increase the financial performance of the company in this case, the setup cost needs to be reduced. There may be any number of reasons why so many parts are scrapped prior to reaching a steady-

Exhibit 8.7   Break-even Price Given Units Sold

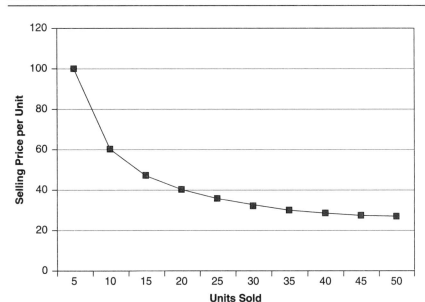

state production rate. If the number of units scrapped is reduced, more time will be available to produce salable units. The cost associated with producing the program will decrease, which can lead to reductions in the necessary selling price to ensure a positive margin. Such a benefit, however, does not require a reduction in prices. This is simply an additional option that is now available to increase demand or market share.

The PM is a much more effective technique to determine the impact of product pricing than is either the contribution margin technique or the full-absorption method. The reason is its use of indisputable data to create information that reflects the reality of the operating conditions of the company. Using the full-absorption method, for example, the true effect of the cost to set up the machine is hidden in a large cost value that includes many heterogeneous costs (setup costs, overhead costs, material costs, and maintenance costs, to name a few). Finally, the contribution margin technique fails to provide the correct information in all circumstances, as simplifying assumptions must be made (allocating action costs, for example).

Endnote

[1]See, for example, Tony Hope and Jeremy Hope, *Transforming the Bottom Line: Managing Performance with the Real Numbers* (Boston: Harvard Business School Press, 1996).

9

Practical Use

Implementing explicit cost dynamics (ECD) is simple in theory. You now understand how costs behave and how they are incurred and can place them into the right bucket so that they can be effectively assessed. This chapter begins to explain the *hows* of ECD. Throughout the chapter, you will begin to understand that the implementation process is one of redefining costs, rhetoric, and measures. It is a different way of looking at almost everything, including the concept of time.

This chapter will begin with a discussion of time. Time and its impact on the organization will be discussed, and common thoughts about time and what the real perspective should be are highlighted. The chapter then discusses common case studies that will show how ECD should be applied in common situations. Finally, general topics associated with the use of ECD in an organization will be explored.

TIME

When managing costs and profits, the most important aspects involve understanding cost and profit dynamics and understanding time. It is generally assumed that time is money; that is, by saving time, money is saved. However, this is only partially true. From a cost perspective, organizations may incur costs over a period of time, such as one hour in the case of a worker's hourly salary. Whatever happens in this hour will not change the cost incurred by the organization. From a revenue perspective, if there is demand for the product, the more that can be sold in a given period of time (understanding that the cost will not change), the greater the profit during that period.

Products and services are a byproduct of what occurs over a given period of time. Costs, by and large, are often very difficult to reduce on a large enough scale to make a real difference. Organizations produce products and sell services to make a profit. They incur costs to design and manufacture widgets, and then they sell them. The issue is what occurs over time. How *long* did it take to design the widget? What is the cycle *time* on machine A to produce widget Y? What is the manufacturing *lead time*? How many machine *hours* are available? How *long* will it take to pay back a particular investment? How many billable *hours* did the consultant work? The information that the organization is most interested in is directly time dependent and indirectly product or service dependent. The key is managing what happens during a given timeframe—this should be the manager's focus.

Instead, managers focus on the unit and the unit cost of a product. Thus, many decisions made at major organizations focus on the margin of an item—a unit. Organizations, in fact, go to great lengths just to determine how much one unit of its product costs to produce. Knowing costs at the unit level is supposed to provide detailed information about the efficiency and effectiveness of a production system and is supposed to be used as a basis for pricing and other decision making. However, there are circumstances where the order and understanding that emerges from a system depends on the robustness and typical properties of the system and not on the details of structure and function.[1] In other words, knowing unit costs does not give an organization more information regarding the performance of the manufacturing system. These unit costs do not converge on one value, so why do organizations place so much emphasis on a number whose magnitude they do not know?

Time Discussions

Many have proposed that time is the critical measure for organizations to manage effectively. One pair of authors, George Stalk and Thomas Hout, suggest that "Senior management must shift its focus from cost to time, and its objectives from control and functional optimization to providing resources to compress time throughout the organization."[2] They continue by arguing that "when a time-based competitor can open up a response advantage with turn-around times three to four times faster than its competitors, it will almost always grow three to four times faster than average for the industry and will be twice as profitable as the average for all competitors."[3]

Christopher Meyer suggests that organizations must refine and introduce products faster than the competition to sustain growth.[4] He goes on to propose that "Shorter life cycles mean that whoever gets there first garners the bulk of the market share while the remainder are left to compete on price."[5]

Focusing on the importance of time, James Blackburn believes that "All performance measures—from the traditional cost-accounting system to newer quality goals—lack an emphasis on speed."[6] Speed, he believes, is important because "From the customer's point of view, what matters is total time required to deliver the product or service."[7]

While the arguments all seem valid, the explanations are incomplete. The rest of this section will describe why they are inaccurately assessing time and a way of thinking about costs and time that will correct the errors.

Why the Disagreement?

The experts are looking at every activity from a cost and cost per unit perspective. Comments such as "Firms find that by removing time from their operations, costs are reduced . . ."[8] and "Common sense suggests that if one can reduce the time it takes to develop a product using the same number of people, costs will drop dramatically"[9] raises questions about whether time is really understood. Likewise, Stalk and Hout (the two authors from before) propose that experience (reflecting the experience curve effect) leads to declines in costs because

- workers and management learn to perform their tasks more efficiently,
- better operational methods are adopted, such as improved scheduling and work organization,
- new materials and process technologies become available that enable costs to be reduced, and
- products are redesigned for more efficient manufacturing.[10]

Units and costs tell very little about the overall activities within an organization because they are a byproduct of specific resource actions. Most costs, however, exist independently of the units that are made. Proof of the independence is the fact that on a Tuesday, for example, the number of units made can be completely different than the number of units on a Wednesday, yet the number of resources may remain the same.

Costs are only one part of the profit equation. Therefore, using costs alone to determine or to assess manufacturing performance is an incomplete measure. By thinking about cost per unit, the issue is clouded even further. Cost per unit thinking causes organizations to consider reducing the machining time on a component from 1.75 minutes to 1.70 minutes because the manufacturing costs per unit will go down under circumstances where costs are allocated using direct labor hours. It also causes organizations to believe that producing in mass quantities reduces the cost to manufacture a product. If this were the case, an organization could theoretically produce an infinite number of products, for instance, and incur no cost per unit. It might also be the reason why many organizations look overseas to produce.

Where the experts diverge regarding ECD is in their assumption that the unit and costs are the center of the operations universe. This is obvious when considering the commonality of the comments made by the so-called experts on time. However, in the limit, units reflect some of the work that was done by resources and nothing else. Costs, similarly, only reflect the financial resources and activities required to run a business. The center of the operations universe should be a bounded relationship between time and profits.

Time provides us with a unifying understanding of operations. Understanding time explains everything from why lean production works, to the effects of poor quality on manufacturing performance, to economies of scale, to whether or not American manufacturers are really saving tremendous amounts of money by building factories overseas and producing in third-world countries.

Whether the organization is considered a time-based competitor or a fast-cycle time competitor, the issue is that the advantages received by emphasizing time are increased opportunities. By improving operations with respect to time, more degrees of freedom are created. More products can be manufactured and sold, and resources can be cut. These activities lead to increased revenues and reduced resource cost, respectively. These are indirect benefits, because after the improvements, an organization can choose not to do anything and, therefore, maintain its existing level of financial performance.

This knowledge of time and its impact on operations is not understood by many organizations. It is widely believed among traditional thinkers that if an organization can design products faster, it reduces its costs.[11] Deschamps and Nayak support this by suggesting the following two reasons for why faster development reduces costs:

1. Increased effectiveness. Wasted time and effort in defining the product, choosing the technologies, freezing the design, dealing with suppliers, and so on are eliminated or minimized.
2. Increased efficiency. Low ratio between development input (number of engineering hours) and output (design volume and quality).[12]

The general belief is that there is no way it can be cheaper to design and develop products two or three times slower. The argument is that time is, in fact, money. If twice the time is spent trying to agree on the specifics of a particular design, it costs extra money. For example, if an engineer who is being paid the equivalent of $25.00 per hour spends eight hours more than expected in design reviews, the assumption is that it costs an extra $200.00. The more time spent doing something, the more expensive it is believed to be.

Costs, however, are not reduced if a product is defined earlier in the product-development process. The engineer will still receive the $50,000.00 salary whether the product is defined in January or June. The benefits of defining the product earlier are increased flexibility later in the development process and shorter overall product-development lead time. The second argument—that of development and engineering efficiency—is similarly inaccurate. Again, engineering efficiency does not directly affect costs; it increases the amount of work that is accomplished in a unit of time. This leads to increased degrees of freedom, one of which is that with additional capacity, an organization can reduce its staff. This is a potential benefit of fast-cycle times, not a direct result. Engineers and a product-development cycle that are efficient are not less costly overall; they just open the number of options an organization will have in the future.

In order to maintain high profitability, organizations must manage costs and maximize program margins and, therefore, the cost recovery ratio (CRR). Under these circumstances, time becomes a key measure along with profit and CRR. Organizations must accomplish the most per unit time while managing what occurs during that time. By managing research and development costs today, an organization can set itself up for maximization of today's profits. By managing what occurs per unit time, organizations set themselves up for maximization of tomorrow's profits. The balance for managers is to manage the costs they incur today while maximizing the amount the department accomplishes during that time. For instance, if an organization can accomplish the same amount of research and development with half the people making the same amount of money as those working for their competitors, this organization may be in a better financial position. Likewise, if an organization can accomplish twice as much during the same period of time, it may be better positioned for the future. Finally, if an organization can produce twice as much with half the people, it is in a much better position than its competitors.

When organizations refer to the cost of doing something, they are sometimes confusing it with the time to perform the activity. However, time does not always mean money. The salary cost paid to an engineer with a salary of $50,000.00 per year is $50,000.00. If the engineer can accomplish twice as much, costs do not go down. A wider range of products might be available to be sold, or a competitor's products might be rendered obsolete more quickly, but the costs involved are still the same regardless of how many products are available or the competitive position of the organization.

Performing an activity faster, therefore, does not necessarily make it cheaper. The only direct results are that activities occur faster and the organization has increased capacity. It is the actualization of doing things faster that is of benefit to the organization. Organizations with engineers that are twice as fast can develop products twice as quickly as their competitors. The result is not lower costs; it is the ability to introduce products to market at such a rate as to make life difficult for competitors. While this can lead to increased sales, it does not decrease costs. The only way to decrease costs in this environment is to reduce the number of engineers. Working with two less engineers obviously reduces costs by $100,000.00 per year. However, working twice as fast does not reduce the amount paid to a particular engineer by $25,000.

So, common sense does not suggest that costs go down when one does things faster; rather, common sense and common math suggest that $50,000.00 is $50,000.00 regardless of what the organization gets for the money. To reduce the costs, reduce the number of existing engineers or pay existing engineers less money. This is common sense.

TIME AND OPERATIONS IMPROVEMENTS

It is often assumed that improvements in productivity lead to cost savings. The cost dynamics and the physics of the situation tell a different story. If a resource can make 10 widgets per hour and the productivity is increased by 20 percent, this person can now make 12 widgets per hour. Many would suggest that there are cost savings in there somewhere. The question is, *where?* Have the costs gone down? No. With more materials used and the labor being the same, the bottom line will show that the costs have gone up. If demand existed for only 10 units, by making 12 units, the organization has reduced its profit. Some may argue that the cost per unit has gone down. The key question is: *What difference does the cost per unit make?* It is not reflected on the bottom line. In fact, the story that it tells is contrary to what happens on the bottom line. Cost per unit is, therefore, a useless measure.

What happens when an organization increases efficiency is that the organization increases its degrees of freedom. These degrees of freedom can lead to improvements but only if they are exercised. For example, with the improvements described previously, the organization has many options. First, it might choose to reduce resource costs to reflect its new capacity levels. It can now make more with the same or the same with less. The organization may choose to reduce the resources to bring the capacity in line with the demand if the capacity is greater than the demand, which will lead to cost reductions. The organization may also choose to continue to operate at the same utilization level so that more parts can be sold. Again, this is not a cost reduction; the improvements come from revenue enhancements. The organization has other options as well. It may now choose to make 10 of the original product and more of another product. This is what efficiency buys an organization—degrees of freedom, not cost reduction.

Assume that an organization can either produce 110 units of product A or 50 units of product A and 50 units of product B. The action costs associated with the production of both products are the same and are assumed to be $1,000.00. The item costs are assumed to be $10.00 for each item built, and the setup costs are arbitrarily chosen to be $150.00. The price of each unit is to be determined. The difference between the two scenarios is that no setup would be required in the former and one would be required in the latter. Assuming operating times for both product A and product B are the same, the setup reduces the number of units that can be produced because of the time it requires. Fewer units per unit time can be produced. The increased number of units that can be produced will increase CRR and profit.

Comparing scenarios, clearly the first scenario has a higher CRR (Equation 9.1). With this scenario, the organization can now afford to lower prices and still maintain the same CRR. Assume that the organization is going to charge some percentage, say x, of the current selling price as the new selling price. CRR_1 would be defined, as found in Equation 9.2.

$$CRR_1 = \frac{110(R) - [110(10) + 1,000]}{OOC}$$

$$= \frac{110(R) - 2,100}{OOC}$$

$$CRR_2 = \frac{100(R) - [100(10) + 1,000 + 150]}{OOC}$$

$$= \frac{100(R) - 2,150}{OOC}$$

$$R = \text{Revenue} \tag{9.1}$$

$$*OOC = \text{Organization Operating Cost}$$

$$CRR_1 = \frac{110(xR) - 2,100}{OOC} \tag{9.2}$$

To maintain the same CRR, the numerators (program margins, or PM) of CRR_1 and CRR_2 must be the same as shown in Equation 9.3.

$$110(xR) - 2,100 \geq 100(R) - 2,150$$

$$x \geq \frac{1}{1.1} - \frac{50}{110R} \tag{9.3}$$

Situation 1. The organization can reduce its price and still maintain the same financial performance as it would have with the two products (Exhibit 9.1). Such a strategy might allow for increased demand for the product. The organization can also choose to keep the existing PM and receive higher profits (Exhibit 9.2). From time savings, organizations have more options that have the potential to increase their profitability.

Situation 2. Assume, additionally, that there is demand for only 50 units of product A and 50 units of product B. The time savings,

Exhibit 9.1   The Original Price Determines the Maximum Percent
Reduction to Maintain Program Margin

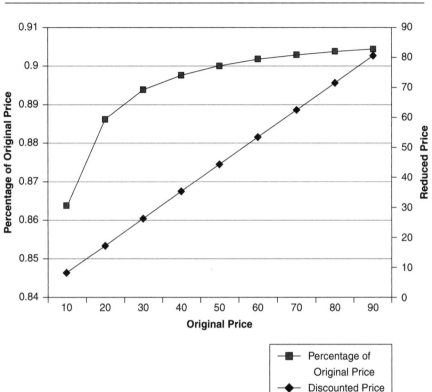

then, would not matter since the additional 60 units of product A could not be sold. Time savings for the sake of time savings does not accomplish anything if it does not lead to increased profitability—regardless of how an organization assumes the cost per unit is changing. Therefore, in a situation such as this, management should shift to driving the total cost surface downward and looking for revenue-generating opportunities (by reducing or selling the excess capacity, for instance).

Situation 3. Because of the flexibility in its organization, the company might be able to provide its customers with the products that they want. The organization might, as a result, be able to charge a premium for the products that it can produce that the more focused operation cannot.

Exhibit 9.2   Comparing Discounted and Nondiscounted PM

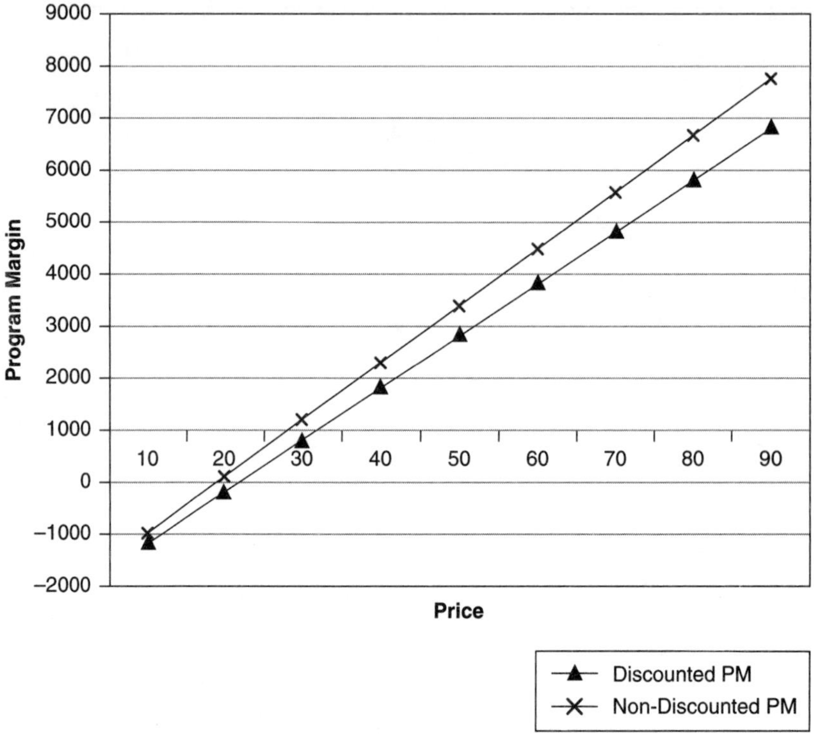

ADDRESSING THE POTENTIAL DANGER OF TRANSFER COSTING

Transfer prices are prices established for the sale of goods or services from one segment of an organization to another.[13] There is an implied transfer of costs from one location to another to represent a purchase of goods or services. It is implied because no costs have left the cost-revenue (C-R) Border. Transfer prices are frequently used when groups within organizations must measure their profitability, and transfer pricing is an easy way to measure departmental performance. Some of the assumptions used to validate the process are as follows:

- Maximizing the performance of each department leads to global optimization of the whole system.
- Measuring a department's profitability is an effective measure of its performance.

Transfer pricing is a dangerous practice, and the reason is simple: Within a multiple-step process, if every step marks up its costs by a profit percentage, the cost rollup will lead to a cost much higher than actual cost. If prices or pricing decisions are based on costs, it is easy for an operation to price itself out of a market.

Consider the following example, which shows the dangers of transfer pricing and implicit cost flows. Department A sells widgets on the market along with training for the customer, which is provided by department B. Departments A and B are both managed as profit centers. The cost of operating department A is $100.00, and the cost of operating department B is $200.00. Organization policy requires department A to package the education with the widget. So, for department B to show a 10 percent profit, it charges department A $220.00 for its services. For department A to bundle the product and the service, its total cost is now $320.00—$100.00 for regular costs and $220.00 for the education of the customer. Department A also must make 10 percent on its sales. Therefore, department A charges the customer $352.00 to make its 10 percent profit.

Assume further that the customer is considering another vendor for the same product. The other vendor charges the customer $340.00, and the customer buys the competitor's product. Department A and department B's organization has priced itself out of a market by accounting for transfer prices and insisting that the departments operate individually at a profit. The total cost for the organization is $300.00. If the organization sells a widget for $301.00, it realizes a $1.00 profit. It could have sold the product for $330.00 and realized, as an organization, a 10 percent profit. The sad reality is that many organizations might argue that they would lose money by selling at $340.00. So, they forgo selling profitable product because they believe that it is not profitable. The result is that they are not profitable because they have sold nothing!

Imagine many departments in the product or value chain having to operate at a profit. It is easy to see how large organizations could price themselves out of markets with such techniques. Clearly, with just a few more steps in this product-delivery process the actual cost of doing business would be very different from the perceived cost.

Many organizations may believe that the transfer-pricing approach leads to global optimization of the entire system. Every department is identifying the value that it adds through its profit. However, it must also compete with outside vendors and competitors. If a department is not competitive with the outside, the organization might even look to other sources to provide the same product or service. Global optimization is not necessarily achieved via independently optimizing all components of a system, however.[14] In this case, emphasizing the maximization of profit each step along the way leads to a perception of costs that is inflated. Given these measures, it is easy to overlook that the two departments work together as part of a system and that it is the profitability of the system—not that of the department—that matters.

The idea of an optimized corporate system or value chain identifies this fact well. As a value-delivering system, no one part is maximized at the expense of the others. All realize that the competitiveness of the system, and, therefore, ultimate profitability, are functions of the effectiveness of the system or the team. The effectiveness is a function of the individual operations or groups that create the value system and also the interactions among these operations. No one operation exists by itself. This is why there has been so much emphasis on identifying cross-functional systems and reengineering them to maximize effectiveness.[15]

Additionally, an objective determination of what effective performance measures are has not yet been widely accepted. However, a measure that can lead to decisions that hurt organization performance when "optimized" should be universally recognized as an ineffective measure.

Transfer prices are not considered costs to the receiving department because no dollars cross the C-R boundary. If a department is providing products or services to another department, there is a general cost to the organization for this ability, which is the cost of operating the department providing the product or service.

It must be noted that transfer pricing does not automatically have to lead to the behavior just described. Robin Cooper cites an example where an organization created fictitious internal dollars that did not impact product price.[16] In this case, the organization ensured that the internal interactions did not affect the *normal accounting process* by separating the systems used to account for dollars. However, such systems are not the norm; therefore, transfer pricing, if used in its more common form, needs to be carefully managed to ensure that negative impacts on the organization's financial performance do not occur.

The bottom line with transfer pricing is as follows: Determining the profitability of each department that makes up a process or a system is not necessary. It does not directly lead to the increased profitability of an organization and can, depending on the situation, lead to poorer organization performance. To determine the efficient operation of departments, performance measures that are relevant to the organization and that lead to a direct (bottom-line) increase in the profitability of the organization must be established and managed.

PRODUCT AND SERVICE RATIONALIZATION

Assume that an organization makes three products. Assume additionally that an arbitrary cost driver is chosen to allocate costs. Across the three products, the costs are allocated as seen in Exhibit 9.3. In this exhibit, the percent of time represents the amount of time, whether actual or estimated, that the cost driver has spent with work associated with that product. Therefore, the resources of this particular cost driver spend 40 percent of their time on product A. Assuming that the resources cost $100,000.00, the technique suggests that $40,000.00 be allocated to product A. If 5,000 units of product A are produced, each product will receive $8.00 in costs from the cost driver.

What if, resulting from a product-rationalization process, it is determined that product B will no longer be produced by the organization? If the now available time is split equally between product A and product C, the cost per unit will change fairly significantly (Exhibit 9.4). What if the products need no additional attention by the

Exhibit 9.3   Cost Driver Allocation Data

Product	Percent of Time	Allocated Amount	Units	Cost per Unit
A	40%	$40,000	5,000	$ 8
B	50%	$50,000	5,000	$10
C	10%	$10,000	2,000	$ 5

Exhibit 9.4   By Tying the Additional Resources to the Existing Products After the Rationalization, the Perceived Cost will Increase

Product	Percent of Time	Allocated Amount	Units	Cost per Unit
A	65%	$65,000	5,000	$13.00
C	35%	$35,000	2,000	$17.50

resources? After all, these products may have been out on the market for some time. This action, then, leads to the increased cost of each product even though nothing has really changed about the product except that the resources now have more time and decide to spend it working on these two products. Additionally, what if the perceived increase in cost per unit causes the organization to believe in the need to increase its prices? The market might tolerate the current price for product C, but if it increases by $12.50, the market might not respond favorably to the new pricing. The organization can, therefore, put itself in a much worse position without understanding why.

It is easy to see that in this example, there were no resource costs saved. The only way to reduce the cost of these operations after rationalizing the products is to get rid of the 55 percent additional capacity that the organization now has. From an ECD perspective, the 55 percent must be eliminated and not moved elsewhere if the organization wants to cut costs through this action. Anything other than getting rid of some or all of the capacity so that the organization no longer incurs the cost will result in no cost reduction. There might be more degrees of freedom for management, but this is not a cost reduction. The increased degrees of freedom that result from the increased capacity might allow the organization to focus on efforts that are designed to enhance overall profitability.

OUTSOURCING AND MAKE VERSUS BUY

Outsourcing has become very popular as organizations look to identify inefficiencies in operations. Outsourcing, however, may have negative effects if improperly justified and valued. Organizations may choose to outsource something because of perceived cost savings that are developed using tools that are ineffective. This suggests that the decision may or may not be beneficial to the organization.

Outsourcing work can be tricky if the cost dynamics are not completely understood. For example, at one college there was a duplicating group that was responsible for large printing programs for the professors and others at the college to use. There was a published price to use this duplicating group. Assume that this price is $0.07 per page. This figure had allocated to it all of the operational costs to run this duplicating group. An English professor realizes that copies can be made at a duplicating organization one block away for

$0.04 per page. What does the professor do? To save money, the professor chooses to go to the duplicating organization so that the college can save $0.03 per page.

The cost dynamics tell a different story. The organization is going to pay for the salaries and the equipment regardless of whether it made copies for this professor or not. Therefore, these are resource costs. By buying the services of this outside duplicating service, the professor actually *increased* costs because the college must now pay the duplicating organization for its services as well. So, what should the organization do? Should it outsource? After all, copying is not a core competence of the college, and perhaps others could duplicate more efficiently. It depends. It is likely that the organization would perform a total cost study. The study would consider the total coordinating cost to meet the needs of the college over a period of time, such as one year. Compared to this would be the expected transaction costs for the anticipated volume of copies. The decision-making process would include answering the question: *What would be eliminated if the college were to eliminate the duplicating group?*

To determine the cost to coordinate duplicating internally for a given copy volume, the organization determines that to meet the expected volume today, it would cost $75,000.00 annually (Exhibit 9.5). The salaries, assumed to be a total of $120,000.00 in this example, are paid by the organization, so the only additional costs incurred are the action and item costs. Much of this can be easily determined. The immediate cost savings are the reduction in action costs and item costs, for they will no longer be necessary if the function is outsourced. This additional capacity increases the degrees of freedom that the organization now has but cannot be counted as savings if the organization is not going to eliminate the cost altogether. If the organization chooses to reduce the resource costs, it can save another $120,000.00, for a total of $195,000.00. These savings will not occur

Exhibit 9.5 Projected Cost Savings for Scenario to Eliminate the Duplicating Group

State	Resource Costs Reduction	Total Action Costs	Total Item Costs	Total Costs
As Is	0	$25,000	$50,000	$ 75,000
Without Group	−$120,000	−$25,000	−$50,000	−$195,000

Exhibit 9.6   To Ensure a Fair Comparison, the Organization Must
Consider All Coordinating and Transaction Costs

State	Resource Costs Reduction	Total Action Costs	Total Item Costs	Total Costs
As Is	$0	0	0	0
Without Group		$10,000	$150,000	$160,000

Exhibit 9.7   Degrees of Freedom Should Be Identified So That the
Decision Maker Understands the Bottom-Line Impact
of all Decisions

State	Cost Savings	Cost	Difference
Eliminate duplicating/ keep resources	$ 75,000	$160,000	$85,000 increase
Eliminate duplicating/ eliminate resources	$165,000	$160,000	$5,000 decrease

if the organization does not take the next step to do something about
the excess capacity.

To determine the transaction costs, the organization may simply obtain quotes on a certain copy volume. The organization must
ensure that it is considering the total cost of doing business the alternative way. For example, if the organization has a person whose
responsibility is to manage the relationship by coordinating activities between the duplicating organization and the college, then
the organization must consider the capacity necessary to manage
the relationship. Additionally, the organization must consider all
of the action costs that are involved. For example, will there be expediting charges? What about transportation and other special
services (Exhibit 9.6)? All of these costs and others must be identified and determined so that a fair comparison can be made (Exhibit 9.7).

The bottom line is that organizations must consider the reality
of the outsourcing situation. On one hand, there is the workforce. To
cut costs, the organization will likely have to cut the workforce. What
impact will this have on employee morale? On productivity? However, no organization wants its employees merrily wandering toward
the unemployment line. Organizations must define, in detail and

with all relevant assumptions, how the opportunity will impact the bottom line. What degrees of freedom will be created? How must the organization act on these degrees of freedom to ensure the necessary savings? These issues, at a minimum, must be addressed to minimize the sure risk that is involved with any such undertaking.

PRODUCT PRICING CONSIDERATIONS USING CRR

The cost recovery ratio (CRR) is a measure that helps an organization understand to what extent a program is paying off the organization operating costs. Because of this, it can actually be a tool to help guide pricing decisions. First, by understanding the cost dynamics, the organization knows the minimum price to ensure program break-even. Above that, the organization may want to determine what the price of the product or service needs to be to achieve a specific CRR. By using the CRR in this way, it becomes a very robust tool that provides managers with a range of information that enables them to make better profit decisions.

The purpose of the following example is to compare the CRR method and the absorption costing method. The comparison would work for any type of allocation-based cost accounting system. Assume, for simplicity, that an organization makes one product. The "costs" incurred over one period are indicated in Exhibit 9.8. Assume 2,000 units were produced and 1,800 were sold. Determine the cost per unit assuming overhead is applied at the rate of $15.00 per hour.

The traditional solution is simple. It involves determining the total manufacturing cost and allocating it to the unit level via the number produced, thus determining the cost per unit (Exhibit 9.9). Overhead is calculated not by the total amount spent by the *resources*

Exhibit 9.8   Cost Data Representing an Arbitrary Organization

Category	Cost
Raw materials	$20,000
Direct labor (1,600 hours)	$16,000
Manufacturing overhead	$30,000
Advertising expenses	$ 6,000
Administrative expenses	$12,000

Exhibit 9.9 Traditional Method for Determining Manufacturing
              Costs

Materials	$20,000
Direct labor	$16,000
Overhead	$24,000
Total Manufacturing Cost	$60,000
Units Made	2,000
Cost per unit	$30.00

and *actions* but by direct labor hours. Therefore, in this case, manufacturing overhead ($24,000) is calculated as shown in Equation 9.4.

$$\text{Overhead} = 1{,}600 \text{ Hours} \times \frac{\$15.00}{\text{Direct Labor Hour}}$$
$$= \$24{,}000.00 \qquad (9.4)$$

In the solution, administrative expenses and advertising expenses for the program are not included. The analysis indicates that any price above $30.00 would pay for the manufacturing expenses.

Material costs are assumed to be $10.00 per unit (assuming all $20,000.00 is spent on units that were produced—that is, there was no scrap). It might be assumed that determining the program margin would be the same as the contribution margin, which would be pricing above $10.00. In some cases it might be, but it really depends. Ultimately, it is important to understand what makes up the manufacturing costs and that action and item costs make up the program administrative and advertising costs. These are costs that must be recovered to make the program profitable. However, in typical analyses, this is not something that the analysts typically spend time understanding. Why should they? As long as it is lumped together, it can be allocated. In this case, assume that there were no other costs associated with this program. Thus, the program margin (PM) would be $11.11, which is different than the contribution margin value because the units sold must compensate for overproduction. Notice that the contribution margin would not distinguish between units produced and units sold (Equation 9.5).

$$\text{PM} = R(U_{\text{Sold}}) - \$10.00(U_{\text{Produced}})$$
$$R(U_{\text{Sold}}) = \$10.00(U_{\text{Produced}})$$
$$R = \frac{\$10.00(U_{\text{Produced}})}{U_{\text{Sold}}}$$
$$= \$11.11 \qquad (9.5)$$

To determine the CRR, divide the PM by the organization operating costs, as shown in Equation 9.6. For stage four profitability, the breakeven, CRR must be equal to 1. Manipulation leads to the relationship in Equation 9.7.

$$CRR = \frac{R(U_{Sold}) - \$10.00(U_{Produced})}{\$64,000.00} \qquad (9.6)$$

$$R(U_{Sold}) - \$10.00(U_{Produced}) = \$64,000.00 \qquad (9.7)$$

With 1,800 units sold (and 200 produced and not sold), this would suggest that the price to ensure breakeven would be $46.67 per unit. Otherwise, the organization operating costs will not be recovered.

One very important issue to note is the following. With the more traditional method, it is assumed that the more products that the manufacturing costs can be spread across, the lower the cost per unit. So, the break-even price for 2,000 units is $30.00. The break-even price for 2,500 units is $24.00. Achieving this cost may help the organization achieve certain cost targets. It might also believe that it could sell its products in the $28.00 range and make a healthy $6.00 profit.

Again, the bottom line tells a different story. The more units that are made and not sold, the lower the PM. Again, more materials are consumed, which the units being sold must recover through pricing. The result is yet another discrepancy between methods. One method, which has results not reflected on the bottom line, suggests that the break-even price goes down as more units are produced (Exhibit 9.10). Another method, which has results that are represented on the bottom line, suggests that they go up. Which will you trust to run your business?

Producing more than is needed is a fairly common occurrence. Consider the following typical story:

> In pursuit of efficiency, Lantech built its . . . machines in batches; it fabricated and assembled 10 to 15 machines of a type at one go. However, because customers usually bought only one machine at a time, the organization had to store most of the machines in a finished-goods area until they were purchased.[18]

Absorption costing does not distinguish between products being sold and products being produced to stock. The distinction is important. First of all, when choosing an arbitrary period for

Exhibit 9.10   Comparing CRR Breakeven to an Absorption-
            Oriented Breakeven

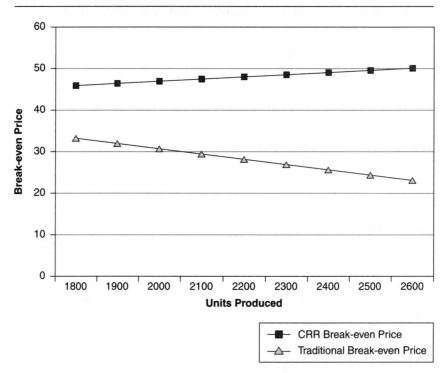

analysis purposes, it is likely that products might be created and not
sold by the end of the period. In the Lantech case, the fact that units
are going into finished goods inventory suggests that time will pass
without units being sold. This will negatively affect the profitability
of periods where units have been produced and not sold. Units produced but not sold contribute no sales to the bottom line, but they
do increase costs (action and item costs exist from the production
process itself). Since none are sold, it does not matter how much of
the fixed costs each unit recovers. Even if one unit can recover all
costs (if sold), if it is not sold, nothing is recovered.

Going back to the example, the 200 units produced but not sold
costs the organization $2,000.00 in materials. By not selling items
that are produced, the organization reduces its profitability by unnecessarily increasing its costs. By increasing those sold, the burden
of each unit is reduced, leading to more options regarding increasing total profitability. Again, organizations that overproduce in the

Exhibit 9.11   The CRR Technique Helps Managers Make Better
Profit- and Price-Oriented Decisions Than Traditional
Techniques

	Absorption	CRR
Cost per unit	$30.00	$10.00 (material costs)
Suggested selling price (*stage two profitability*)	>$30,000	>$11.11
Price to ensure aggregate profitability (*stage five profitability*)	>$30.00	>$46.67

name of efficiency reduce their profitability and tie up resources that
should be used to make products for which there is demand.

The ECD and the CRR equation provides more management
information although it does not determine a unit cost. However, it
does accomplish the following:

1. It identifies the various types of costs (resource, action, item).
2. It identifies the costs in such a way that managers have an
   objective knowledge about which costs are affecting
   profitability and how.
3. It provides unambiguous information. It determines the price
   necessary to recover organization operating costs, what price
   allows for different types of break-even, and the effects of any
   other cost on the bottom line of the organization (Exhibit
   9.11). The $30.00 figure carries less information about the
   financial effects that it will have on the organization.
4. The CRR takes into account all costs and revenues over an
   arbitrary period so that the requirements for profitability are
   easily determinable.

The key concept in this chapter is that the cost per unit should
not be a determining factor in any management decisions. The areas
of focus as you make decisions and run your business should be time
and profit and the interaction between the two. How can you use
time advantages to make more effective profit-oriented decisions?
This is the only way to ensure that your decisions have truly measur-
able bottom-line impacts.

Endnotes

[1]Stuart Kauffman, *At Home in the Universe: The Search for the Laws of Self-Organization and Complexity* (New York: Oxford University Press, 1995), p. 19.

[2]George Stalk, Jr. and Thomas M. Hout, *Competing Against Time: How Time-Based Competition is Reshaping Global Markets* (New York: The Free Press, 1990), p. 37.

[3]Stalk and Hout, *Competing Against Time*, p. 37.

[4]Christopher Meyer, *Fast Cycle Time* (New York: The Free Press, 1993), p. 7.

[5]Meyer, *Fast Cycle Time*, p. 7.

[6]James D. Blackburn, ed., *Time Based Competition: The Next Battleground in American Manufacturing* (Homewood, IL: Business One Irwin, 1991), p. 23.

[7]Blackburn, *Time-Based Competition*, p. 17.

[8]Blackburn, *Time-Based Competition*, p. 8.

[9]Meyer, *Fast Cycle Time*, p. 29.

[10]Stalk and Hout, *Competing Against Time*, p. 6.

[11]See, for example, Jean-Philippe Deschamps and P. Ranganath Nayak, *Product Juggernauts: How Companies Mobilize to Generate a Stream of Market Winners* (Boston: Harvard Business School Press, 1995).

[12]Deschamps and Nayak, *Producing Juggernauts,* pp. 59–60.

[13]See, for example, David H. Marshall, *A Survey of Accounting: What the Numbers Mean,* 2nd ed. (Homewood, IL: Irwin, 1993), p. 446.

[14]See, for example, Eliyahu M. Goldratt and Robert E. Fox, *The Race* (Croton-on-Hudson, NY: North River Press, 1986).

[15]See, for example, Michael Hammer and James Champy, *Reengineering the Corporation: A Manifesto for Business Revolution* (New York: HarperBusiness, 1993).

[16]Robin Cooper, *When Lean Enterprises Collide: Competing Through Confrontation* (Boston: Harvard Business School Press, 1995), p. 285.

[17]Adapted from David H. Marshall, *A Survey of Accounting: What the Numbers Mean,* 2nd ed. (Homewood, IL: Irwin, 1993).

[18]James P. Womack, Daniel T. Jones, and Daniel Roos, *The Machine That Changed the World* (New York: Harper and Row, 1994), p. 142.

10

Implementing Explicit Cost Dynamics

This book has focused on the theories and concepts of explicit cost dynamics (ECD). This last chapter, which will introduce ideas associated with implementing ECD, provides guidelines only—not a detailed plan. With the knowledge provided in the book as a basis, desirable ways of implementing the concepts can be established in time.

Implementing ECD involves the following four issues:

1. Organization, preparation, and program implementation
2. Establishing the relationship, if any, with currently used costing methods
3. Information systems design
4. Establishing the right measures, language, and plan to ensure long-term acceptance and success

This chapter will examine each of these four areas and will present recommendations regarding implementing the concepts.

ORGANIZATION

When implementing ECD, it is essential to first understand how the organization operates from a cost management perspective. Many organizations are deeply attached to the existing cost management systems, leaving them unable to change to more effective systems.

This attachment to the cost accounting system creates all levels of behavior, from individual measures and incentives to process performance and scheduling all the way to the higher levels of management. In cases like this, implementation involves much more of a focus on change management and on having the upper levels of management totally committed to driving an understanding of the cost and profit dynamics of the organization.

The specifics of the organization and how it operates will impact the personality of the ECD framework implementation. An organization without control, for example, may find itself unable to implement ECD with the necessary rigor to ensure value for the organization. Specifically needed for the implementation is an understanding of the organization's philosophy; the goals, objectives, and strategy; and the organization's measurement and incentive program. The organization must also have an effective plan for the design, development, and implementation of programs. Without an understanding of these concepts, it is unlikely that the magnitude of the impact that is possible from a robust implementation will occur.

Philosophy

In general, ECD is a flexible concept. It can be used in any organization regardless of industry, products, or services. It simply explains the cost dynamics of an organization's environment and provides a framework for measuring activities and improvements to those activities. The difficulty with implementing ECD, however, lies in the facts that

- the paradigm created by traditional cost accounting, including activity-based costing (ABC), is difficult to break because of its extensive use and acceptance over time, and
- the measures and metrics driven by traditional accounting exist throughout and are deeply ingrained in most organizations.

Breaking the Cost Accounting Paradigm

There should be no question that a strong paradigm has been created by cost accounting. When asked whether it is cheaper to make ten widgets than five, most people would automatically answer yes and would be puzzled if you asked why. Most would suggest automatically that time is money without even questioning the concept. Breaking the cost accounting paradigm in organizations will require a focus on the facts of cost and profit dynamics and strong leadership from all levels in the organization. Focusing on the facts will help eliminate the subjectivity associated with selecting and using a cost management system. When organizations understand that the traditional accounting systems do not represent the bottom-line cost and profit dynamics, it is hard to justify why decisions should be made in the absence of knowingly real and accurate information.

With an ECD framework, strong leadership will be required from multiple levels within the organization. Upper management must tell the story of why ECD is being implemented and must be fully committed themselves. Middle management must understand that there is no trick to ECD and that the effective implementation focuses on what is good for the organization. Finally, the workers throughout the organization must focus on ensuring that the techniques are properly implemented and that they effectively measure the desired attributes so that the organization can more effectively manage its costs and programs.

Overall Measures and Metrics

Cost accounting–oriented measures and metrics exist throughout most organizations. The leadership must question whether the measures are appropriate in terms of creating and supporting the desired behavior throughout the organization. If the measures do not cause the desired behavior, regardless of how ingrained they are, the measures must be replaced with tools that compel the organization to move in the right direction.

It is recommended that at some level the measures coexist in the form of pilots so that managers can see the impact of the measures on performance. This will allow for organizations to begin to plan the part of their decision making that might run counter to existing measures.

Goals, Objectives, and Strategies

When considering the implementation of ECD, it is important to assess where the company is and where it is going—a time-phased approach. Knowing where the organization is not only will help the decision makers identify where they are operationally but also will identify how close they are to their ultimate goals, how rapidly they are achieving their objectives, and what strategies need to be employed to ensure that the firm successfully navigates its path toward its desired space. ECD itself should not be a goal, an objective, or a strategy. However, when developing the goals of the organization, financial managers should use ECD as a foundation for managing cost data.

People Measures and Incentives

From an operational perspective, it is important to understand how an organization measures performance and how it provides incentives to its human resources and the human resource managers. At a high level, measures and incentives must be driven by upper management, which will ensure the following:

1. *The entire organization understands that the executives are behind the effort.* This is especially important when dealing with a framework where many of the measures used to manage seem to run counter to those used for many years. Executive support will make it seem acceptable to reduce the utilization on a machine in order to ensure profit increases.

2. *The executives who are at a high enough level to be impacted by measures on their respective organizations must drive the implementation of the measures and must ensure convergence with desired behavior.* Those at the highest levels in the organization can often see what the desired behavior is and can influence the implementation of the right measures to ensure the desired performance. Managers should resolve those conflicts within their areas of responsibility to ensure that measures do not contribute to poor performance for the organization.

3. *Organizational interactions must be considered so that territorial disagreements do not lead to suboptimal performance.* One of the hardest tasks for an organization is to manage the interactions between functions, groups, or people. Executives, however, owe it to themselves and to the organization to understand the cost dynamics of a situation and to work together to ensure that territorialist behavior does not impact the performance of the organization. For example, marketing and operations are often in conflict when it comes to sales and operations planning. Sales might make bigger and, from an operations perspective, unreliable forecasts. Operations might be forced

to work with this forecast or, as is often the case, might change the forecast to what it believes is realistic. The result is frustration between the groups and an overall lack of trust. These are the types of issues that need to be addressed by the organizational owners responsible for ensuring smoothly operating programs.

PROGRAMS

All activities that organizations perform require programs. The programs collect organizational and cost data and information for the purposes of managing the organization's resources and activities. More specifically, programs focus on

- understanding the work that is being done by the resources,
- understanding the time that the resources are spending doing the work, and
- understanding how and why the organization incurs action and item costs.

Understanding the Work

Each day resources spend their time engaged in activities ranging from productive work to doing nothing. Each X-hour day is comprised of a set of activities. The question is, does management know what work is actually being accomplished in an organization as a result of these activities? Too often, the answer is *no*. The work of resources is often hidden in the organization, its hierarchy, and its accounting, which reduces, and often eliminates, visibility into what is being accomplished by the resource. Therefore, a machine or a person can exist in an organization and can work on a task, and others have no visibility into what the resource is accomplishing. Because managers will not understand their production capacity and how to effectively manage it, they will be prevented from making decisions that can increase the profitability of the organization.

Resource Time

Resources perform the work of the organization. The time and capabilities of the resources define the capacity of the organization to do its work. The organization, therefore, must be able to effectively understand and plan the time that resources have. If the organization has too much capacity, managers must be informed of the situation to allow them to act accordingly. The organization might seek additional work to meet its capacity, or it might choose to reduce the amount of capacity that it has. If it does not have enough capacity, decisions must be made regarding how to choose the right work to optimize what the capacity contributes to the organization's performance. Either way, organizations must have objective visibility into their capacity so they are able to make decisions that will ensure the desired organizational performance.

Incurring Costs

Organizations incur costs as a result of, or as a driver of, their work. In other words, an organization's resources define its capacity. The resources incur costs through performing actions that involve explicit costs or by procuring items that involve money leaving the organization. The reasons that organizations incur these costs must be understood fully if costs are to be effectively managed. Therefore, by tying action and item costs to the program, organizations will be able to understand how each cost at each level is incurred, for what reason, and how it impacts the performance of the organization.

So, when managing the organization, programs are a key attribute to understanding and managing organizational activities and performance. Programs allow for the tracking of action and item costs and tracking of resource utilization, and they create the information basis for organizational improvement. To effectively manage programs, the following three necessary management components must be considered:

1. Creating programs
2. Program measures
3. Program management

Creating Programs

The management of processes and programs is likely to involve fairly significant changes in the organization. This is because the process for managing all programs involves being able to capture the item and action costs associated with the program itself.

Getting Started

As organizations look to improve their understanding of overall cost dynamics in general and program costs in specific, the question is, how does the organization begin? The goal is both to ensure overall improvements and also to begin to develop the capabilities of the organization to implement the concepts. Ultimately, the organization should look for two things. First, the immediate large opportunities for improvement should be sought. This will allow the organization to use the concepts to identify opportunities for improvement. By identifying these opportunities, the organization will have positive reinforcement with regard to the use of the techniques and also will show how the techniques can create overall value in the organization. Second, when capturing the costs, the organization must be able to identify the cost types and cost levels and must ensure that the costs are explicit in nature. Only then can the organization be assured that the recommendations will allow bottom-line impacts to occur.

Creating New Programs

When creating new programs, the details surrounding the program must be understood. Not identifying the details of the program can lead to either not capturing costs, which can happen if holes exist between programs, or double counting them, which can happen if two programs overlap. The program scope, therefore, must be well planned and articulated to ensure that everyone working within the program and in adjacent programs knows where the programs begin and where they end. Who incurred the costs and for what reason must be defined up front as well as possible to ensure that the cost dynamics of the program are well understood. Without this understanding, costs may be captured incorrectly, leading to cost dynamics that do not accurately reflect the activities within the program. Finally, resource utilization is critical in planning capacity and in understanding the demands of the program. How resources are attached to the program is a very important issue to manage.

As programs change over time, managers must redefine and articulate the scope to ensure complete understanding of what the program has become. Similarly, costs and resources must be updated as necessary to reflect the changing program.

Program Measures

The latter half of the book focused on the various program measures that are used with ECD. These are the measures that the organization will use to understand the bottom-line impact created by the program. To recap, as a result of their normal activities while heading toward specific results, programs incur item costs and action costs but not resource costs.

Item Costs

One of the key data values is the item cost. It is important to attach the relevant item costs to the program without allocating costs. How is this done? If the items were purchased specifically for the program, the program owns the cost. For example, if a builder buys a specific door at the request of a client, that door can be considered an item purchased for the program created for that client. However, if the builder buys doors in anticipation of demand, the doors are resources that are to be used when the demand comes and are therefore not applied to the programs as program costs.

Action Costs

Action costs, too, must be carefully considered when applying them to programs. Actions that span two or more programs that are not tied to a superprogram become resources and are managed as such. Additionally, it is important to only count actions that impact the cost dynamics of the organization. The organization should not apply an implicit cost to the cost of a program. The organization cannot decide, for example, that actions performed by a resource during 10 percent of its time costs the organization 10 percent of the resource's salary. This is simply not true and defeats the purpose of ECD.

Handling Resource Costs

The cost of resources cannot be applied to programs. Their time for utilization purposes is applied so that managers can understand the demands of the program, the capacity of resources, and also how resources spend their time. However, the cost is not applied because the costs exist with or without the program. Resource costs, although separate from programs, are equally important in terms of managing costs. Organizations must be able to translate resources into capacity so that capacity management becomes an activity based on facts rather than anecdotes.

Program Management

The key to managing programs is in understanding how the program fits into the organization overall. This is important because decisions regarding capacity and resource utilization and how costs are incurred should be tied to a bigger picture, which should create the context for decision making. This will keep managers from arbitrarily cutting costs and assuming that this will automatically lead to global benefits. Program managers must manage costs and must ensure that the management tools reflect the reality of their situations. They must ensure that their decisions have the desired bottom-line impact from a program cost perspective and a program margin perspective.

Program Cost

As organizations look to identify ways to improve performance, the program will be one of the key areas on which efforts should be centered. Within the program, resource utilization is captured and costs are captured. The costs captured in the program are tied directly to the bottom line so the bottom-line impact of each cost-oriented decision is immediately known. Managers must manage the program costs effectively to allow the organization to effectively manage its overall costs. This is especially difficult given the multidimensional nature of costs. However, because costs are linear, monotonically increasing functions, it becomes easier for software or even hand calculations to provide the necessary information so that the cost dynamics are understood. It will be important for managers to always understand the program cost dynamics and to manage the programs with the idea that the purpose is not to reduce costs. Rather, the purpose is to ensure profitability, partially through the management of program costs and their cost dynamics.

Contribution to Profitability

Managers must always understand the impact that their programs have on the bottom line. Unlike internally facing programs, where there is only a cost component, externally facing programs have a profit component because they have a revenue component. It will be important to always understand and manage the cost dynamics and the profit dynamics, which will be accomplished by using the program margin as a way to ensure that the program itself is profitable for the organization. Additionally, managers can use the cost recovery ratio as a way to determine the rate at which programs are recovering the resource costs and internally facing costs that the organization incurs. With this measure, organizations can, for example, compare the cost recovery ratio for multiple programs or look at the aggregate cost recovery ratio for a period. Either way, the purpose is to understand the immediate impact on the bottom line of externally facing programs.

A note of caution: Having an arbitrary minimum cost recovery ratio is not a recommended practice. Any positive cost recovery ratio suggests that costs are being more than recovered. To suggest that programs that fall below a certain arbitrary value are not worth pursuing because the value is not high enough may not generally make sense. The only times where this might be an issue is in a resource-constrained environment where the organization must make the most money that it can or in a situation where the organization is focusing on premium pricing to develop a certain brand image in the market.

COST MANAGEMENT

Coexistence with Cost Management Techniques

There might be a question regarding what the relationship between ECD and other cost accounting systems might be. Can the methodologies coexist? Can ECD use any aspect of the current cost accounting system? After all, the cost accounting paradigm is very strong, and many organizations have spent a tremendous amount of effort and time to develop the system that is currently in place. This investment and the resulting organizational behavior creates commitment to the concepts. The answer to the question of coexistence in this case is: it depends. It depends on a number of issues, so each major cost accounting methodology and activity-based management will be discussed.

Standard Costing

It will be difficult to salvage much of what an organization has with its standard costing system. The basic philosophy is simply focused on determining the standard cost of a product, which has been shown, is impossible to determine. The reasons for the difficulty are as follows:

- The system itself is a technique based on allocating fixed costs.
- Standard costing focuses on cost reduction rather than profit optimization.
- Because of the ultimate responsibility of an operation within a process, the need for standards themselves is in question.

Allocating Fixed Costs

The concept of allocating a fixed cost to determine a unit cost violates the primary premises of ECD. First, allocating costs creates an *understanding* of costs that is inconsistent with the law of conservation of dollars. Doing more cannot cost less, but the implication created with a cost per unit rationale is that costs do, in fact, go down with volume. Second, the cost uncertainty hypothesis argues that a cost per unit cannot be determined because to do so would require an arbitrary allocation. Given the number of allocation techniques that exist, it can only be assumed that a unit cost is indeterminable. The concept in and of itself does not make sense. How can one set of inputs operated on by a mathematical function create multiple outputs? This violates the fundamental law of functions in mathematics (one input yields one output) and is simply flawed logic. Logically, only one cost per unit should be calculable. Therefore, any of the thinking associated with trying to determine a unit cost through allocating must be eliminated to effectively implement ECD.

Cost-Reduction Focus

The idea of reducing costs is fine when it does not interfere with profit-oriented thinking. The assumption that cost reduction always enhances long-term profitability is incorrect. For example, if the owner fires everyone, sells the assets, and goes home, how much money will the organization make in the long term? None. When applying the thinking to more plausible and realistic situations, the logic often still applies. Cost cutting in the absence of understanding the revenue and therefore profit impact can limit an organization's ability to make money. Infrastructures needed to build, sell, and deliver products and services can be damaged or completely broken when focusing on costs, which can lead to the inability to generate revenues. The correct view is one that includes revenues and costs together so that an assessment of the profit impact of cost reductions and even of cost increases can be determined.

Validity of Standards

Standards can be of use in some circumstances, but when focusing on them, the organization's degrees of freedom vis-à-vis operating parameters are limited. The idea of operating at a rate less than standard is not acceptable because of the cost implications of doing so. However, operating at standard can actually limit the profitability and flexibility of an organization. Production rates should reflect the needs of the operation. If an operation capable of five parts per hour needs to operate at three parts per hour because it has excess capacity, so be it. Standard costing, however, does not support this philosophy.

Activity-Based Costing/Management

Activity-based costing (ABC) is considered to be less arbitrary than standard costing. The drivers of the fixed costs are identified and are salient when using ABC. For this and other reasons, some of the infrastructure that exists with an ABC system can be maintained with an ECD implementation. However, the following reasons for why the systems can be implemented together still exist:

- The concept of a cost driver can be used to understand why resource costs exist and how they are utilized.
- Use of activity-based management (ABM) can help understand program management costs.
- ABM can be used as a management technique that focuses on operational improvement.

Using Cost Drivers

Organizations must be able to manage their costs and must be able to understand the impact of changes to costs on their overall profitability. The idea of the cost driver and the techniques used within ABC to analyze cost drivers can help organizations understand their resource utilization and their program costs. In fact, some organizations might want to use the concept of cost drivers as a first step to understand some of the cost dynamics in the organization. Caution should be taken, however, to ensure that explicit costs are being analyzed and that they are not allocated to the cost of a unit. These costs often exist independently of the units that an organization produces and are not allocable.

Using Activity-Based Management for Program Management

Activity-based management (ABM) is an excellent technique for understanding how an organization and its resources spend time and efforts so that the cost dynamics in the organization can begin to be understood. The recommended approach to allow ABM and ECD to coexist would be to first use the aspects of ABM to understand how pools of resources spend their time and then to use that information to begin to understand what programs exist within the organization. Once this is known and once the programs have been defined, ABM can be an approach used to manage the programs in terms of capturing costs and providing relevant feedback to those managing the program.

Focusing on Operational Improvement

If ABM is used as a management tool, once it is in place and steadily operating, it can be used to create organizational improvements. For example, organizations might be able to identify areas of excess capacity or limited capacity by looking at the activities of the resources that make up the capacity. Decisions to increase or decrease capacity can then be made to ensure operational and financial improvements.

Using ABC by itself, however, will create challenges for the following reasons:

- ABC is still an allocation-based technique. No matter how it is sliced, the purpose of ABC is to determine a cost through allocation and, therefore, should be avoided for this use.
- The math of ABC does not reflect the reality of cost dynamics. As mentioned with standard costing, allocating costs violates the fundamental concept of cost and profit dynamics.

The bottom line with integration is that ABC and ECD are not a good fit. Since ABC is mathematically the same as standard costing, it has the same inherent problems of standard costing. ABM, however, can coexist when implemented within the ECD framework.

Theory of Constraints

Much of the ECD framework somewhat reflects the theory of constraints (TOC) cost management concepts developed by Goldratt. The reason for this is simple. TOC begins with the premise that organizations are in business to make money. This being a given, managers must simply measure how to make money and then effectively manage the organization to create profits. ECD shares this philosophy. Second, TOC is really a packaging of optimization ideas and techniques that have been effectively developed, expanded, and articulated in a way that makes sense to an average person. An example is the drum-buffer-rope (DBR) system for operating manufacturing. If the attributes of the operation being modeled were input into a linear programming solver, the result of how a business should be operated to drive profits would match Goldratt's suggestion. However, Goldratt has helped us understand how to schedule and how to manage to that schedule with DBR, synchronous manufacturing, and TOC cost management. Had Goldratt packaged his ideas and presented them as traditional optimization with extensions, he would have failed. The assumption with ECD is that the same optimization solutions that are assumed to be true with TOC are also assumed to be true with ECD.

For organizations using TOC, ECD can be used as a logical extension of the TOC implementation with the following considerations:

- The concepts are fairly similar. ECD focuses on profitability and true optimization.
- TOC is based in optimization, as are some of the concepts in ECD. True optimization means solving a problem, which is limited or impacted by constraints and not by the overused notion of improving a metric.
- Those who practice TOC would be able to accept the paradigm of ECD. Forward-thinking individuals who have accepted TOC should have a smaller shift to ECD than those who focus on allocation. To accept TOC suggests that the

fundamentals of allocation-based costing are incorrect. ECD provides extended capability, techniques, and understanding beyond that typically found in a TOC implementation.

- Restructure costs and cost types from TOC cost types to ECD types. To ensure the full effectiveness of ECD, cost types such as throughput, inventory, and operating expenses should be replaced with the traditional ECD cost types of resource, action, and item costs. This will provide the granularity necessary to implement ECD and to have it provide the relevant information.

SYSTEMS AND TECHNOLOGIES

Information Systems

ECD is highly reliant on information—sometimes highly complicated information—for its decision making. Because of this, information systems support can greatly aid in capturing, storing, and analyzing the data required for ECD to work. As of this writing, however, no ECD software exists. Some organizations might want to add ECD functionality to their existing system. Other organizations might want to write ECD capabilities in the software that they sell as the concept becomes more prevalent. In either case, some basics should be considered to help influence drive the design and implementation of ECD software.

The system and its architecture are very important; although the ECD aspect of the system is not transactional, it relies on transactional systems to capture its data and feed the database that it will use for analysis purposes. Therefore, the modeling and program management needs of ECD would need to be designed into the setup and operational aspects of the transactional modules or, at a minimum, there must be knowledge regarding what transactional data will impact the data needed for ECD analysis.

Going back to the fundamentals of ECD, accounting modules of a system are very important. Money flowing into an organization defines revenue, and that money is handled on a transactional basis by an accounts receivable software module or accounts receivable functionality. It will be critically important for ECD to be able to capture these data for use with its analysis of revenues and profits. As the accounting software identifies revenues and places them into the right revenue buckets, ECD must be able to understand the transaction and must be able to tie the transaction and the timing of the transaction to the program that drove the revenue. This will help determine the program margin and will ultimately determine the cost recovery ratio.

Accounts payable has similar responsibilities. ECD needs to understand when money leaves the cost-revenue (C-R) Border. When making payments, ECD will want to know what is being paid, when and to whom it is being paid, and what program is driving the cost. Every payment that leaves the organization should be tied to a program so that the total cost of the program can be determined. With these data, information about the program and its effectiveness will be more easily attainable for management.

The general ledger (GL) is potentially a very important source of data for ECD. Given the fact that many of the financial transactions that occur end up populating the GL, the GL tables can provide much of the data required for not only initial cost analysis but also for ongoing analyses. The GL tables may have the raw cost data that the ECD module and its queries can use to populate its own tables for the requisite cost type, cost level, and program management functionality. Within the GL, accounts have been created—when identified and understood—that can hold the data representing the items, actions, and resources that are involved in the management of the organization. To understand program costs, therefore, would involve the identification of one or several GL accounts that hold the cost data for that particular program.

The accounting database is probably the key component of an ECD system. Having an effective and easy-to-use database is a key criterion to effectively manage ECD programs using software. Also, the organization should build the ECD capabilities on the same database that is used for all of the accounting data. This will make development, operation, and ongoing maintenance much easier for the organization. Typically, enterprise resource planning (ERP) packages will capture their transaction cost data and other operational cost data into the accounting and ledger tables of the database. Having this information in a database makes it more easily accessible, which can aid in its usefulness. Maintaining a database will also allow for data to be more easily and effectively linked and queried. Querying is very important, especially when performing cost dynamics analyses or what-if analyses that are critical for planning cost dynamics scenarios.

When designing a system for use in the organization, it makes sense to use the existing database and to completely follow the appropriate protocol defined by the organization for proper data integrity. For example, an organization will not want data that are captured by the financial modules of the software to be changed by the ECD module designed by the organization. The ECD module should be able to query the data from the financials database and use these data for its own analysis; however, it should not be able to change the data and place them into the same location from which they were taken. Additionally, if programs themselves incur costs, the population of the database resulting from the items and actions of the program must enter the database through the transaction capabilities within the enterprise's system.

Program Creation

Organizations must have a method for creating and managing costs. The easiest way would be to have software, software modules, or overall functionality that would manage programs and program identification information and would be used, along with the transaction system, to capture costs, update the database, and query the database for program management information. From a resource management perspective, resource and resource time would be assigned to the program. This is not to capture resource costs or to assign resource costs to the program, for this is not how ECD works. From a resource perspective, it is only for the purposes of managing utilization. The organization would know how many and what resources are or were assigned to the program. When kept in the database, this information would allow for queries against the use of resources on programs as well as how a resource is spread across programs.

In application, it would be possible to define a program, assign resources to the program, define expected item and action costs (or use those that have been defined elsewhere and are usable within this particular functionality), and define the expected items and actions to create both an estimate and a baseline for the program itself. The software would then be responsible for the capture of costs through interacting with the transaction system and updating the database. Actuals would be available, which could help the organization to understand such information as baseline versus actuals for the purpose of better estimating and to identify opportunities for improvements. The organization could also seek to understand the capacity of the resources and how effectively the resources were managed by looking at the output of the group and the costs incurred. The caution here is that this work should be done to promote overall profitability. Those responsible for the implementation should stay away from the temptation in this case that more is better. Instead, the managers should try to focus on understanding exactly what the program should accomplish and what is required to accomplish it— no more and no less. The organization should then manage the resources to accomplish this task in the most productive manner. The goal is to stay away from contests to get the most done given the resources, for accomplishing too much with a program might suboptimize the operations of the whole organization.

Capturing Cost Data

Cost data should be captured by a transactional system, but the data must be made available through the database. The types of data desired center on capturing the actual item and action costs associated with the program. For example, as the information is captured for the actual transaction, information about the program can be captured as well. Thus, for all transactions associated with accounts payable or accounts receivable, a required entry should identify with which program the transaction is associated so that all costs and revenues associated with that program are recognized and available for management analysis and future reference. This technique will help ensure that all of the transactions are managed by the transaction system, which will maintain the integrity of the system and the management of information. It will be very important to capture the actual costs not so that the organization is positioned to take punitive action for missing the estimations for the original projections for the project but to use the information to learn how to more effectively understand ECD, how to estimate programs, where the hidden costs might be, and to identify risk and risk mitigation–oriented issues.

Program Metrics

The programs and the software used to help manage the programs must be able to use the ECD measures to evaluate the program and to analyze cost and profit dynamics. Since costs are multidimensional functions, software with deep analytical capabilities and reasonable mathematical capabilities is required. Instead of getting a graphical representation of the organization's cost dynamics, it might be necessary to make assumptions to simplify the number of dimensions. For example, if the resource costs were held constant at a value of X, what would the total cost be given Y actions and Z items?

The software must capture the right revenue values and the right item and action values so that the total program costs and program margins can be determined. Additionally, through querying the accounting database, overall break-even information along with total cost and cost recovery information can be made available.

Managing Costs

The idea of managing costs with the system should be a relatively straightforward task once the system is in place. With the database, all information associated with the costs of the program are immediately available. Therefore, querying a particular program should deliver all item costs, action costs, total program costs, the periods in which the costs were incurred, interprogram item and action costs, and the list goes on. Managers must keep in mind multiple issues when managing costs.

1. *When setting up the system, the cost types must be assigned at the relevant cost level.* Costs are not to be assigned to just any level. If a cost is incurred for two or more programs, for example, that cost should either be assigned to a higher cost level (superprogram) or should be considered a resource cost. An example would be shipping products from two different programs on one truck. Although the normal tendency would be to allocate the costs to both programs, this is wrong. While the math is easier, it does not reflect the true cost dynamics of the situation. Instead, the shipping can be considered a higher level action cost, for the capacity being purchased (for which two programs are being shipped) is a resource that the organization can use.

2. *Always keep in mind the true cost dynamics.* Program managers have the responsibility to manage the programs. They must understand the contribution that their program is making and must manage the cost of making that contribution. Programs will incur costs that will affect profits for the period. Managers must understand how costs are incurred and what their overall contributions are so that the costs can be managed effectively.

Cost management does not mean cost reduction. Rather, cost management means making the right decisions from a cost perspective to ensure short-term and/or long-term profitability. Managers may manage costs by reducing unnecessary costs just as they may increase costs to increase the capacity of an organizational constraint. It is important to understand the relevance and salience of the cost so that the proper decisions can be made.

3. *Understand the multidimensionality of costs.* Total costs and total program costs are multidimensional. There are many independent costs that make up the cost surface that exists in an n-dimensional space. Decisions should be made not by oversimplifying the cost model to make it representable from a graphical perspective but by using the querying and reporting tools to understand the impact of decisions on the cost dynamics of the situation.

Reviewing and Analyzing Costs

Throughout the period and the program and at the completion of the program, the organization should review the cost dynamics of the program to ensure that it met all of the predefined objectives. There must be a never-ending desire to learn how to manage and use costs to ensure the types of products, services, and growth that the organization desires. The objective is not necessarily to cut or reduce costs; instead, the objective is to use costs to effectively create profits. So, if an organization sees from experience that raising costs can increase the cost recovery ratio, it may want to increase costs until it finds that costs are increasing at a faster rate than revenues. At that point, cost cutting becomes an issue. The key is to have the data that will show the impact of the program that caused the increase in costs.

A review of the data over time helps the organization close the loop between the program and ongoing results. Often when a program is completed within an organization, it is gone forever. When this happens, the relevant information needed to assess why something happened is no longer available or the circumstances driving the decisions that were made are no longer available for analysis. Organizations must not let this happen by documenting the dynamics of the programs themselves and by regularly circling back to the program and its outputs to ensure that quality work is always being done.

Getting Started with Existing Data

A significant amount of data often is already available to the organization to help the process of analyzing cost dynamics. The organization has been collecting its information into its GL and its database for some time, but how does the organization use what currently exists to help with the process of understanding cost dynamics? These data can be used to begin to look at program costs, overall cost drivers, and how well resources are being utilized so that improvements in operations and cost management can be made. From an ECD perspective, the data used must be able to provide the desired information. Therefore, the following key questions must be considered:

1. Are the cost data usable?
2. If not, how can they be cleansed?
3. How does the organization update and maintain the data?

Are the cost data usable?

From the cost data collected by the organization, can explicit costs be identified? How the financial systems handle intracompany transfers and other types of nonexplicit costs might present a difficulty. Are these cost data intertwined with the explicit costs? Can explicit revenues be identified? Is there enough information to determine the item and action costs? These are the types of questions that must be answered to determine whether the cost data will be usable so that organization of the data can occur for analysis purposes.

If not, can they be cleansed so that they can be used by ECD?

More than likely, the organization's data will not be in an ideal form. There might be many causes for this. For example, the accounts that were originally set up in the system might create a situation where explicit and implicit costs are both captured into the same account. In cases where the data are not perfectly aligned with the data required by ECD, the organization must understand what the assumptions were behind the development of the accounts that are being used by the current system. This might provide some insight into which data could be used for an initial analysis. Certain data points might be usable if their origin is known to the extent that it can be determined whether the cost is implicit or explicit. If this information is available, it should be used as a basis for an initial cost assessment. Otherwise, the organization will need to begin capturing the data that can be used in another format. Ultimately, the organization will need to be able to identify explicit costs for future analyses.

How does the organization maintain and update the data?

The transaction system should be responsible for the continual updating of the database, and the organization should strictly adhere to this design rule. Pure maintenance of the data should be handled by the system resources to ensure that data and information management and product upgrades and expansions are much simpler tasks.

ENSURING A SUCCESSFUL IMPLEMENTATION

Implementing ECD is not a trip or a journey. A trip suggests that there is a plan, a beginning point, and an end point. ECD does not have an end point. It involves incorporating a new lifestyle—a mode of operating. It will become a part of the organization's DNA and will form part of the basis for corporate evolution. Getting to this point, however, requires a significant amount of work from many throughout the organization. To effectively implement ECD, organizations must seek and manifest

- the right attitude,
- the right measures,
- the right language,
- the right plan, and
- the right value proposition.

The Right Attitude

An organization interested in implementing ECD must focus on the real cost dynamics of the organization. The concern is on creating a reality about what is happening within the organization from all perspectives—day-to-day, period-to-period, and program-to-program. The right attitude means that leaders will seek the truth in managing their organizations. They seek to drive overall value for their employees, their customers, and their markets.

The Right Measures

The right measures focus on bottom-line values and the measures driven from them to ensure that management understands the bottom-line impacts created by their programs. The measures focus on what comes into the organization and leaves the organization in the form of revenues and costs, respectively. All financial measures used to assess organizational and program performance should be directly tied to the bottom line so that there is no loss of information when trying to understand how an item, an action, or a resource will impact the bottom line. The measures are also tied to revenues so that decisions are not made in a vacuum.

The Right Language

Cost per unit is a dead concept. Anything associated with allocation, too, is a dinosaur. Instead, the key areas of focus should center on ensuring bottom-line impacts. The issue is not how to cut costs; the issue is how to manage costs to ensure improved profitability. Cost dynamics, explicit costs, cost uncertainty, bottom-line impact, programs, program margins, multidimensionality, profit dynamics, cost types, and cost levels should be the topics of conversation for an organization. The right language will help organizations focus their efforts on doing the right thing from a financial perspective.

The Right Plan

Once ECD has been implemented, leadership should not tolerate in any way the old view of cost accounting. Managers should not allow employees to talk about allocating costs to programs or the concept of *cost per something*. It will take a while to get to this point; in fact, the organization may want to sample its culture by implementing pilots or prototypes so that the issues with the particulars of a culture can be identified early on. However, once ECD is up and running, cost accounting will be dead and should rest in peace without employees trying to bring it back to life.

The Right Value Proposition

Each organization will determine the value proposition of ECD. Implementing ECD will not lead, in and of itself, to bottom-line impacts. The value proposition is that it increases the number of degrees of freedom available to organizations in terms of managing costs and factors that can increase profiles. The value proposition also is that it will help managers understand, in great detail, how the organization has performed, is performing, and will perform. It is not a financial value proposition. It is one that will, without a doubt, allow managers and organizations to operate in ways that they have never seen before.

Index